THE PRINCE

NICCOLÒ MACHIAVELLI

The Prince

Translated, with an Introduction

by

A. ROBERT CAPONIGRI

A Gateway Edition

HENRY REGNERY COMPANY · CHICAGO

TRANSLATOR'S PREFACE

The present translation has been made, in the main, from the edition of *The Prince* by the late eminent Italian historian Federico Chabod (Niccolò Machiavelli, *Il Principe,* Introduzione e note di Federico Chabod, Torino Unione Tupografical Editrice, Torinese, 1927, Collezione di Classici Italiani, Vol. XXXV). However, occasion has been taken to compare his readings with those of such other editions as Schillero's (*Il Principe ed altri scritti minori di Niccolò Machiavelli,* a cura di M. Schillero, Milano, Hoepli, 1916), Osimo's (*Scritti politici scelti di Niccolò Machiavelli,* a cura di V. Osimo, Milano, 1916), Lisio's (*Il Principe di Niccolò Machiavelli,* a cura di Giuseppe Lisio Firenze, Sansone, 1900), and Burd's (*Il Principe by Niccolò Machiavelli,* edited by L. Burd, Introduction by Lord Acton, Oxford, 1891). The outstanding merits of Chabod's text are evident. He did the definitive work in establishing the date of composition of *The Prince,* resting his case both on external evidence and on minute analysis of the text, the results of which have proved most valuable for the edition. In addition, he has adhered to the Machiavellian orthography and other textual details with great fidelity.

The translations of *The Prince* into English are many; all have value and each has been conducted on principles which the translator deemed important and necessary. The controlling principle of the present translation has been taken from Machiavelli himself. In the dedication to Lorenzo the Magnificent, Machiavelli writes of his book: *lo quale opera io non ho ornata né ripiena di clausole ampie, o di parole*

*ampullose o magnifiche o di qualunque altro lenocinio
o ornamento estrinseco . . . perché io ho voluto o
che veruna cosa la onori o che solamente la veritá
della materia e la gravità del sogetto la faccia grata"*—
"which work I have not adorned nor filled with roll-
ing phrases or magnificent and impressive words or
any other extrinsic attraction or decoration . . .
because I have wished that either nothing at all or
only the truth of the matter and the seriousness of
the subject should make it outstanding." This has
been transposed into a norm in the present instance.
The entire central purpose of the translation has been
to make the truth of the matter and the seriousness
of the subject come through to the English reader.
To achieve this, fidelity to Machiavelli's own style
has been necessary. That style is a complex one,
wholly reflecting the diverse formation and experi-
ences, mentality and intentions of the man himself.
It is a "tough" style: direct, concrete, unadorned;
marked by involutions designed to carry nuances of
thought and reference; sinewy and masculine, in
places even rough and earthy. It is also capable of
elegances and even of strong, virile imagery, as for
example, that of comparing fortune to the mountain
torrent, recalling Vico's great analogy of history as the
fresh water of the past flowing into the salty seas of
the present. To know Machiavelli's thought, then,
it is necessary to catch at least some of the flavor
of his style, a thing which the present translation has
carefully sought to preserve. As a consequence it is
not "modern," nor "interpretative," nor "idiomatic,"
nor any of the other things which other translations
have tried to be. It is as nearly as possible simply
Machiavelli with all of the original characteristics
of the man and his style, coming through in English
garb. My hope is that whoever reads these pages, will

experience a flow of ideas through an authentic voice from the past, speaking of things our generation can ignore only at its peril. Further, my purpose is to bring to the reader something of the true accents of that voice, so he can form for himself a living image of Machiavelli, the man: worldly, idealistic, sage, simple, prudent and naive, experienced and innocent, consumed by the one desire to achieve direct vision of reality: *vedere come stanno le cose.*

A. ROBERT CAPONIGRI

CONTENTS

INTRODUCTION

The Prince was composed, as Federico Chabod has established, in the year 1513. At this time its author was in a period of disfavor. The previous year on the accession to power of the Medici, he had been dismissed from his post as secretary to the chancellery, or governing senate, of the Republic of Florence. Thwarted in his political and civil career, Machiavelli had retired to his small property in the hills about Florence. From his terrace, we are told, he could just discern the outline of the city towers and walls, a circumstance which could only have peopled his imagination with restless images of all that was transpiring in the halls of state from which he had been banished.

The frustration of his personal ambitions had effects, however, which were far beyond his intent and which only subsequent ages would be able to evaluate. Ever an energetic man, Machiavelli turned his enforced leisure to the composition of those works with which his name is ineradicably linked in the history of Western thought. In their composition his intent was direct and simple. He would set down, for the utility of those who might understand, the wisdom in political and civil matters which he had garnered from the years of his own experience and from the unceasing perusal of the ancients. But Machiavelli wrote larger than he knew. His works indeed encompassed his first intent. Far more than this, however, they revealed him as the interpreter of his own age and the prophet of a new age; indeed, he deserves the encomium of the philosopher Gioberti, who referred to him as the "Galileo of political thought."

To know the mind of Machiavelli is to know the mind and the spirit of his age, the Renaissance, in a particularly direct and intimate manner. Indeed, he expressed his own intention, in *The Prince,* in a phrase which might well stand as the rubric of the entire age: "andare drieto alla verità effettuale delle cose"—to penetrate to the effective truth of things. It is this intent which establishes that affinity with Galileo which Gioberti rightly recognizes.

The Renaissance has appeared to some in the rather pathetic guise of a forlorn attempt to revive the glories of an ancient past. By certain external trappings it might superficially be judged so, just as Machiavelli, from his adulation of the ancient great, may well create the impression of one whose vision is turned to an inimitable past. A direct consideration of the man and of the age, however, reveals immediately how superficial such impressions must be.

If anything, the Renaissance is an age turned, not to the past, but to the future. Its animating spirit is not the recall of an age that is past but the sense of the power within itself to create a new age, one such as the world had never seen. An undue emphasis on this futurism, however, must also distort the image. The Renaissance is interested neither in the past nor in the future. Its interest is, as Machiavelli expressed it, in effectual truth, in what things, events, man, God, history, nature, truly and effectually are; in their authentic and abiding being. The Renaissance was in its innermost essence the effort of western man to strip his vision of all the myths, fancies, theories and projects which had heretofore clouded it and to confront reality and to name it for what it is, under its basic and enduring character. The truth of this observation is not denied, but only made humanly pathetic, by that fact that in this effort the Renaissance created myths, visions, shibboleths of its own which veiled reality from view as effectively as any that had gone before. Nevertheless, the spirit of the Renaissance remains the will to effective truth, the surrender of illusion. Its myths testify only to the fact that it too was the work of man.

The Renaissance turned the full beam of this will to effective truth in every direction and in its light revealed the world in aspects it had never exhibited before. Directed upon nature, that will to effective truth steadily dissolved that animism which had before invested it, paving the way for the modern view of nature and the achievements of modern science. Turned upon man, it revealed him, as Pico says, in his "most elegant oration upon the dignity of man" both in his heights and in his depths; touching at the one extreme the heights of heaven, at the other the most primitive and base elements of earth; but above all, in his *central* character, as the point at which earth and heaven meet and are effectively united in the great works of the human spirit. Turned upon society, it revealed it as the arena in which man's towering egoism and his all-inclusive altruism, his soaring idealism and his almost insensate will to power engage to create historical, institutional forms the constitutive principle of which is tension. Turned upon religion, as the philosopher Giovanni Gentile has noted, that light revealed it as at once the potential source of man's most profound illusions and the one principle without which his life is nought, his work meaningless, and his own being a self-negation. Finally, that will to effective truth revealed history to man as the theatre of his effective creative energy, the arena in which all that he saw of the effective truth of things might be translated into the effective principles of works of human expression: art, events, institutions, projects.

To attribute this will to effective truth to the age, however, is something of a figure of speech, that figure by which the character of the immediate and the concrete is transferred to a projective whole. The "Age of the Renaissance" is in the last analysis an abstraction. If it can be said to possess this character or trait, it is because the men of that age, singly and collectively, possessed it. It is from Machiavelli, and the other effective voices, that we draw the spirit of the age. On the whole, the area in which Machiavelli sought this effective truth may be said to be limited in the range of human concern to the political order. That it is a central area, however, no one would care to deny. Just because of this concentration, moreover, Machiavelli was able to press this inquiry more forcibly.

What is the effective reality of the political order? What are the principles which explain it, as Galileo might have said of the phenomena of nature, *juxta propria principia*, in itself, according to its own constitutive elements? How might these principles be transformed from mere observations and explanations into insights and rules, the science into an art? These are the questions in which his will to effective truth took concrete form. The answers he formulated are documented by his works; above all, or at least in a very special and intimate manner, by *The Prince*. As a consequence, who knows *The Prince* knows Machiavelli, just as one who knows Machiavelli comes to know his age, directly and intimately. For this reason, we may turn from the age and from the man to the work.

What is it in *The Prince* which justifies the universal conviction of its relevance for our own day? The answer to this question is difficult to formulate for two reasons: the peculiar character of the work itself and the ambiguous cloud of interpretation which has accumulated about it in the course of the centuries. Machiavelli, and in particular his *Prince*, have with the course of time become veiled in a cloud of myth so dense as to obscure the reality completely. Before the real relevance of his thought for the twentieth century can be appreciated, this veil must be dissipated. It may help to indicate just what the Machiavellian myth has been, and what the reality might be which will stand revealed when that myth is dispersed.

The Myth

The myth of Machiavelli and of his *Prince* is not simple, but complex. It is a double veil, woven of myth and countermyth, forming an intricate fabric. The original may be called the "demonic" myth; in it Machiavelli, and precisely the Machiavelli of *The Prince*, appears as the incarnation of the immoral will to political power. Over against this must be set the secondary myth; it may be called the "heroic." In it, the Machiavelli of *The Prince* appears as the melancholy Hamlet of the world of political reality, castigating in ironic and satiric vein the immoral will to power in man, while delineating an esoteric doctrine of freedom. He is seen as the prophetic forerunner of a cause which only four centuries later was to emerge above the waters of history: the liberation and unification of Italy. Both myth and countermyth have

power to arrest the imagination, and possess truth,
each in its own one-sided way, as all myths do. But
neither singly nor together do they render present to
us the real Machiavelli or the real significance of his
Prince.

The image of Machiavelli and of his *Prince* according to the demonic myth is fixed for the English-
speaking mind in the many passages in English literature, and especially the literature of the Elizabethan
period, in which it has been projected. Mario Praz
has brought these passages together for critical study
in his fascinating work *Machiavelli and the Elizabethans;* but the passage from *Henry VI* of Shakespeare
may well represent them all;

litany of infamies

Why I can smile and murder while I smile
And cry Content to that which grieves my heart
And wet my cheeks with artificial tears
And frame my face to all occasions;
I'll drown more sailors than the mermaid shall;
I'll slay more gazers than the basilisk;
I'll play the orator as well as Nestor,
Deceive more slyly than Ulysses could;
And, like a Sinon, take another Troy.
I can add colors to the chameleon,
Change shapes with Proteus for advantages
And set the murderous Machiavel to school.

"The murderous Machiavel": this is the clear and
concise depiction of the original, the demonic myth,
of Machiavelli; and the fact that it brings to culmina-
tion this litany of infamies in Shakespeare's passage
points up the lurid implications of the epithet. It is
in line with this myth that some have traced the
familiar name of the devil himself—"Old Nick"—to
Machiavelli's own Christian name, Niccolò.

The genesis of this myth is not too difficult to trace. It derives, in the first place, from a rather literal and unimaginative reading of the text of the *Prince*. Its context is the classical conception of the relation which ought, ideally, to prevail between the realms of ethics and politics. According to this classical conception, which was of Greek origin, refined and elevated by contact and fusion with the Christian gospel, politics had been conceived as a science subordinate to ethics. This relation held even for Aristotle, who defined man as "zoön politicon"; for this designation implied only that ethical ideals can be realized only in the context of human fellowship; it did not in any way imply autonomy for the area of political action. Ethics inquires into the supreme ends and values of human life and action. It indicates the unconditioned norms for the pursuit of the good life. Politics, by contrast, defines a limited, though supremely important, area of the pursuit of the good life. It is concerned with the disposition of social forces in the manner most consonant with the attainment of the good life. Its whole office, like that of the art of government, is to create, ideally, the conditions under which the values indicated by ethics might be achieved. Politics, consequently, both as science and as art, was unequivocally subordinate to ethics. As a science it draws from ethics its first speculative principles, according to the laws of that hierarchy of the sciences which Aristotle had so carefully elaborated. As an art—the art of government—it draws from ethics its first principles of action. Under the speculative aspect, politics appears as a subalternate science to ethics; under the practical aspect, the relation between them might best be described as instrumental. This conception, with its roots in the highest intellectual achievements of the western world, had endured for two thousand years, and was held to be but the reflection in the science and discourse of man of an eternal order of truth.

This is the conception which *The Prince* of Machiavelli appeared—to a literal reading—to deny and to dislodge with subtle logic and a brutal realism of fact. In its place, Machiavelli would seem to have erected an idea of politics as a science and an art which would be intrinsically independent of ethics, if not its simple negation. Politics appears to be presented not simply as autonomous but actually superior to ethics in the pages of *The Prince*. While ethics dwelt in the empyrean of the ideal, of the "ought to be," *The Prince* of Machiavelli moved in a world of cold fact, seeking only to penetrate and order the reality which imposed itself imperiously upon man, the reality within him—his own nature—as well as the reality without. Such a science, such an art—without equivocation a science and art of the real—must surely be superior to a science which dwelt only upon the ideal, the "ought to be." Such was the impression created by the direct and literal reading of *The Prince*. But such an impression, viewed against the background of the classical conception, could only appear as a monstrous distortion and the mind which projected it, a veritable incarnation of demonic malice. Hence the image of the "murderous Machiavel"—an image embracing indifferently the man and his doctrine.

Over against this demonic myth stands the heroic myth of Machiavelli. Its origin is also readily discernible. Its roots lie in a desire to displace the demonic myth, and to redeem Machiavelli from the obloquy of centuries. The demonic myth is relatively simply in outline; but the heroic myth is much less so. In it, several strains are interwoven to complicate its pattern. In the first place, the classical conception of the ideal relation between ethics and politics was shared as much by those who sought to redeem Machiavelli as by those who had stigmatized him. This imposed a sharp limit upon the available means of rehabilitating him. This rehabilitation had to be effected without challenging the frame of reference within which the demonic myth had arisen, without violating the classical theory of the transcendence of ethical over political science. To this end, several paths were attempted.

The first and most effective perhaps was the "historical" reinterpretation of Machiavelli and of his *Prince*. The demonic myth had lifted Machiavelli and *The Prince* out of historical context. It had confronted his doctrine directly with that of the classical tradition. It could do this because the classical mind conceived of truth as eternal and transcendent, essentially independent of the limitations of time and place. The historical interpretation seeks to evade this confrontation by reintroducing Machiavelli's doctrine into its historical setting. By this strategy, it hoped to show that all that must be stigmatized in Machiavelli as depraved might be traced to the depravity of the times and not to the author's intent. Even more, it hoped to display a dual level of intent in *The Prince*: one reflecting the influence of the depraved times, the other the pure ideal, wholly conformable to the classical conception, which Machiavelli really held and which he was defending, by the literary instruments of irony, satire and sarcasm. In this effort, the historical interpretation was materially aided by the very real possibility of contrasting the doctrine of *The Prince* with the thoughts and sentiments expressed and espoused in other of his writings, such as the *Discourses*, the *Histories* and the *Legations*. In these latter works, Machiavelli would seem quite unequivocally to have espoused a republicanism of an aristocratic cast very reminiscent of the classical and especially the Roman sources, breathing a spirit of freedom and virtue which recalls the Gracchi as it seems to forecast the heroes of the Risorgimento.

The doctrine of *The Prince,* this historical interpretation argued, cannot be made to stand alone. It must be made to relate, in a direct or indirect manner, to this other Machiavelli, who is clearly as authentic as the Machiavelli of *The Prince.* Where find the principle of this relation? Obviously, in "the times." The republicanism, the spirit of liberty of the *Discourses,* represents the "true" Machiavelli, speaking what he really believed. *The Prince* represents his concession to the political and moral depravity of his times, or it represents a satire upon the times, employing the classical device of the *reductio ad absurdum.* The incommensurability between the normative, the ideal, and the historical and actual is notorious, and none has suffered from it more than the philosophers, from Plato forward. Little wonder, then, that a philosopher should give vent to his exasperation with the actual situation in his own time by depicting its most lurid details in satire and even by the device of lifting those lurid details to the status of a mock ideal. This, then, is *The Prince:* Machiavelli's pitiless rendering, by satire, irony and sarcasm, of the conduct of political life in his own day; a pattern which by all his ideal standards is a travesty of the political life of man. Concrete evidence to support this interpretation is drawn from the political situation of Italy at the end of the fifteenth and the beginning of the sixteenth century, and the political "mores" of the times. The ruthlessness of political action, the bitter protest against foreign occupations and usurpations, the dim but haunting dream of an Italy *"libera e civile"* (in a phrase made classical by Machiavelli himself, and echoed in our own day by his profound student and apologist, Benedetto Croce) and perhaps one and united from the Alps to the Straits of Taranto, are all interwoven to make the argument compact and concrete. From this interpretation *The Prince* emerges as a document of rare complexity—at once an ironical and satirical commentary on the political situation of the day, a masterpiece of invective cloaked as praise. Machiavelli himself stands revealed as a noble figure, committed to the classical conceptions and ideals, but embittered by the depraved times in which it was his lot to live. He merely dissected the political savagery he saw about him, closing his account with an apostrophe to the ultimate liberation of Italy which recalls the opening lines of the Virgilian eclogue. This is the countermyth of Machiavelli complete.

Because it keeps speculation close to actual existence, the historical interpretation of a doctrine is always attractive. In the case of Machiavelli, it is especially appealing, for it brings together the diverse elements in the Machiavelli record into a plausibly coherent whole and depicts the writer in a noble guise which arouses a warm and spontaneous admiration. At the same time, it remains far from persuasive, for it contradicts irrepressible characteristics of Machiavelli's mind and work, *The Prince* in particular. In the first place, *The Prince* is indubitably "theoretical" in the classical sense of the term, despite whatever historical elements may shine through the text or may, by external research, be brought into connection with it. Machiavelli's mind is singularly free of that historical orientation of which the historical interpretation of his work is the product and which is so characteristic of our own day. He would have repudiated any interpretation of his work which orientated it principally toward the circumstances of his own day and away from the "true principles" of political action. This is established by the conception of history which Machiavelli reveals in his work, in the Florentine histories and in the *Discourses*. It is the characteristic conception of the Renaissance: the function of history is to teach by example, and what it teaches is not contingent fact but universally true principles of human action. This is the reason why Machiavelli could use Livy as the "peg" upon which to hang his own doctine of liberty. This attitude shines through the text of *The Prince* itself; its contemporary observations and analyses, so acute and penetrating, are made to support not contingent recommendations, but universal maxims. To construe it otherwise is to misconstrue it. The historical countermyth of Machiavelli fails, with the original or demonic myth against which it is directed. While it renders him a more sympathetic figure, it drains him of all force and vigor, denying to his utterances their one claim to our attention: universal validity.

What, then, is to be done, in order to arrive at a just estimate of *The Prince* and its doctrine, an estimate which would enable us not only to report its content but also to derive its significance? In the first place, it would seem, one must abandon myth and countermyth alike, for both distort our vision of Machiavelli. Yet, we cannot abandon them completely. There is a germ of truth in each which is the basis of its plausibility and of its power, and this element of truth must not be lost. The fact is that the task of interpretation is more difficult than either myth would lead us to suppose. It is necessary to synthesize, and not to set in opposition, the historical and the theoretical elements in Machiavelli, that is, those elements which relate to the circumstances of his time and those which claim the universal authority of truth. In this way an image of Machiavelli will be achieved which is, after all, the true image of every thinker—the image of a man, fettered by time, seeking to enunciate a truth which is eternal.

The Reality

The historical interpretation of Machiavelli is right in seeking to link him and his doctrine with the concrete events of his time, for, abstracted from such attachment, man is a ghost. It is mistaken, however, in the choice of the historical order to which it seeks to attach him. It links him with the ephemeral political transformations of his time. Important as these are, they still do not form the context of his ideas. He belongs rather to the history of thought and ideas, and, more specifically, to the history of western man's effort to understand the nature of political life and its relation to ethical values. When placed clearly in this context, the false antithesis which established myth and countermyth alike—the historical versus the theoretical Machiavelli—disappears. It is replaced by the image of the historical Machiavelli addressing the profoundest, perennial problems of political philosophy. Philosophizing in the context of his own age, he projects into new relations and new light the basic problems of politics and of ethics. Read in this association, the text of *The Prince* can be interpreted with strict literalness and assigned at the same time its full historical and philosophical significance.

Prior to the appearance of *The Prince* the areas of ethics and of politics had not been clearly discerned

at the theoretical level. The autonomy of the sphere
of political action had indeed been recognized practically; that is to say, man acted politically, whatever
theoretical justification he may have advanced for
his actions. This political action, analyzed diversely
from the political and from the ethical points of view,
presents profound contradictions. Prior to Machiavelli, such analysis was not possible on clearly ascer-
tained theoretical grounds. The contradictions were
felt, but not theoretically grasped or clarified. The
universal persuasion stood for the transcendence of
ethical over political values. At the same time, however, at the level of action, the pressure of circumstances and the necessities of political action, the
ipsis rebus dictantibus of Roman law, against the
limits of ethical theory made itself felt. The inarticu-
lately discerned problem was this: how could the
autonomy of political reality be recognized without
releasing it from the overarching control of ethical
principles? This was the problem, felt, but never
clearly enunciated in Western thought before Machiavelli. And it is the clue to the positive and indisputa-
ble achievement of Machiavelli. He for the first time,
posited this problem in a striking manner, by docu-
menting, in the Prince, the general form of the principles of autonomous political action.

What then was the form and source of the confusion, or more precisely, of the lack of distinction between the ethical and the political areas in Western
thought before Machiavelli? The former, obviously,
is more readily determinable than the latter, but they
are quite obviously linked closely. The confusion was
twofold. In the first place, there was lack of distinction at the theoretical level between the universal and
normative propositions which constitute the enuncia-
tive form of ethics and the limited, hypothetical and

"positive" propositions of political science. Ethics is controlled by the normative ideal, universally valid for all men, at all times, in all places because it is based not on the observations of the fluent circumstances of history but upon the scrutiny of man's "nature." This ideal is expressed in propositions of universal but non-existential import. Human action, however, does not transpire at the ideal level; it takes place at the level of the transient, the contingent, the problematic moment of human existence. It is, consequently, orientated toward the strategies of existence in such circumstances and these strategies demand a wisdom quite proper to themselves, a science which would yield the immediately relevant imperatives of action. Thus man's thought seems distended between two opposing forces. Again, the form of the confusion appears as the tension between the ideal moment and the moment of force. The greatest legacy of ancient wisdom was its ideal of reason: that reality is rational and that human action likewise is orientated toward reason and may become permeated by the rational principle. This orientation toward reason stands in opposition to the fact and the moment of power which is simply the human will as yet unmediated and transformed by reason. Man is distended between these moments as he is distended between the necessary and the contingent, the universal and the particular. The moment of force is simply his existential state, and this can never be resolved, without residue, into reason—the ideal toward which he moves.

Classical thought, before Machiavelli, thus presented the aspect of seeking to resolve the moment of contingency into the necessary, the particular into the universal, the moment of force into the moment of reason. In the particular area of human action this involved the reduction of politics to ethics. Of course, there is the saving thought that human life could exhibit the synthesis of these factors and not the absolute transcendence of one over the other; but classical thought suggested no unambiguous principle for the effective synthesis of these dimensions of human awareness. If, on the other hand, we seek the source of this confusion, it may, with a certain degree of confidence, be said to reside in the overweening attachment of classical thought to the one and the abiding—an attachment so strong that through Plato it could place in Western thought the seed, destined ever to germinate, of the idea that the realm of the contingent, of the particular, of force in human action, is in some manner unreal.

This most dangerous tendency was, however, constantly counteracted and limited by the insistent testimony of existence, by the stubborn fact, as Whitehead would have called it. It is this fact that the historical interpretation of Machiavelli emphasized when it construed the doctrine of *The Prince* as a commentary on the times. For the fact which this interpretation emphasizes is certainly true, namely, that while all during the period of classical thought the unity of ethics and politics had been affirmed theoretically, practically men had continued to practice the art of politics as the science of the contingent in human affairs. The historical interpretation of Machiavelli is, consequently, entirely in the right when it insists that his doctrine contained nothing that was really new—that it merely recognized the state of things as they were. Translated into more cogent terms, this emphasis places Machiavelli in the correct light. It is thus possible to say that he is taking a significant step toward clearing up the centuries-old confusion, or lack of distinction, in Western thought between ethics and politics, between utility and morality. And this is the first canon for the interpretation of *The Prince.* It is the first unequivocal recognition in Western thought of the autonomy of the political and, through the political, of the moment of utility, in human action, in the sense that this moment cannot be resolved, without residue, into the moment of morality, as classical thought had imagined.

When viewed in this light, it is clear in what the positive character of *The Prince* consists. It contains the first lineaments of a philosophy of power. And its first step is to isolate, for better identification, the object of its concern—power in its political form as manifested in overt political action. Machiavelli is too profound, however, to undertake to demonstrate that power—the moment of power in human action—is autonomous, that its particular physiognomy can never be identied with that of morality. He makes this axiomatic. This it is which gives the breathless daring and the almost pure geometrical form to the progress of his argument. Given that power is autonomous, the theorems, the corollaries, the scholia proceed with limpid clarity and irresistible force. There emerges a pure philosophy of power embracing a delineation of its inner character, a technique of its deployment and employment, a strict science of its dynamics. And this it is which the reader will find, naked and unashamed, in *The Prince.*

This source of the logical clarity and strength of *The Prince* and of its unshakeable position in the history of modern thought is, at the same time, the source of its weakness and profoundest confusion. Its strength was the axiomatic affirmation of the autonomy of the moment of power, the assertion that it could and must be dealt with in no derivative terms, but only in terms originative and constitutive of its own character. But how does such autonomy differ from isolation? Are we not to conclude from this the complete fragmentation of the human spirit, the complete isolation of its constitutive moments from each other? And is not such fragmentation the radical denial of the spirituality of man? To these questions Machiavelli, at least in *The Prince,* has no direct answer. The fact is that he did not possess the resources for the resolution of these further problems; he had exhausted himself in his heroic affirmation of the autonomy of power in politics. He bequeathed to later generations, consequently, an equivocal heritage—a doctrine which cannot be questioned in its basic assertion but which cannot be accepted in its stark isolation. And with this, he bequeathed a fresh task, that is, the achievement of the unity of the human spirit by the redefinition of the principle of synthesis among its constitutive moments. More specifically, he has left us the perennial task, in new and more forceful terms, of defining the positive relationship between ethics and politics, conceived now as two positive moments of the human spirit, which demand resolution in the higher reality of the unity of the human person.

This problem modern thought has taken up with resolution, if not with unequivocal success. Its most complete form is that of the relation of thought and action in man. And of this wider problem, the question of the relation of politics and ethics is a more specific determination. To indicate what positive resolutions to this problem have been advanced by modern thought is not, of course, the purpose of a simple introduction to *The Prince.* It is sufficient to say that the very existence of the problem in this form is the chief historical monument to Machiavelli's importance in the tradition of Western thought.

It is the chief proof, finally, of the view that *The*

Prince is of greater significance for our own day than it was for Machiavelli's own. For through the intervening centuries, this problem has become ever more urgent for Western man as the scope of his action and the instruments at hand have increased, until, finally, in our own time, we appear to have reached the ultimate, with the potential destruction of the human race within our grasp. We are all, consequently, despite ourselves, Machiavellians, not in a doctrinal sense, but in the problem we confront. This is why *The Prince* can never be dislodged from its place among the imperatives of our civil education.

A. ROBERT CAPONIGRI
Notre Dame University

NICCOLÒ MACHIAVELLI
TO
HIS MAGNIFICENCE LORENZO DE' MEDICI*

Those who wish to gain favor with a prince most often approach him with those things from among their possessions which they hold most dear or in which they see that he takes delight. Hence it is that princes are frequently presented with horses, arms, cloth of gold, precious stones and similar ornaments, worthy of their exalted station. Desiring in my turn to present myself to Your Magnificence with some testimony of my devoted service to you, I have found nothing among my possessions that I hold more dear or that I esteem so much as the understanding of the actions of great men, which I have acquired through long experience in contemporary affairs and continuous study of those of antiquity. After having diligently examined those actions and meditated upon them for a long time, I have brought together the results of these efforts in a small book, which I now present to Your Magnificence. Although I consider this work unworthy to be presented to Your Magnificence, nevertheless I am confident that your understanding of men will lead you to think it worthy of acceptance. For you will understand that I could have offered you no greater gift than an instrument which will make it possible for you to understand in the briefest span of time, all that I have come to know and understand through the labor of so many years and with so many personal afflictions and dangers. I have not filled this work with high-sound-

* For all proper names see the glossary of names.

ing phrases, with magnificent and impressive words, or any other kind of extrinsic attraction or ornament with which many writers are in the habit of decking out and adorning the matters with which they deal; because it has been my wish that nothing else should distinguish the work and make it acceptable save the variety of the material and the seriousness of its subject. Nor, I hope, will it be considered presumptuous that a man of such humble degree and low estate should venture to discuss and to suggest rules about the manner in which princes should govern. For just as those who design or paint landscapes take their position below in the plain, to consider the form of mountains and uplands, while to consider the form of low places they place themselves high on the mountains, so, in order to understand well the character of peoples, one must be a prince, while to comprehend well the nature of princes, one must be a man of the people.

Accept, therefore, Your Magnificence, this little gift in the same spirit in which I offer it. If you will read and analyze it diligently, you will recognize in it my intense desire that you should indeed reach that exalted station which fortune and your other endowments promise. And if Your Magnificence, from the summit of your lofty position, will sometimes turn your eyes upon these low places, you will recognize the degree to which, against my deserts, I bear with the great and unrelenting malice of fortune.

I

How Many Kinds of Principalities There May Be and the Ways in Which They May Be Acquired

All the states, all the forms of government, which have had and do have dominion over men, have been and are either republics or domains subject to princes. Principalities, in turn, are either hereditary, in which the bloodline of their lord has for a long time constituted the ruling-house, or newly established. In like manner, the newly established principalities are entirely new, like Milan established by Francesco Sforza, or they are like members joined to the hereditary state of the prince who has acquired them, like the Kingdom of Naples in relation to the King of Spain. Domains acquired in this latter fashion have been accustomed either to living under a prince or to being free. And they are acquired by a prince either with the armed forces of others or with his own, either by favor of circumstances or by his own personal capacity.

II

Hereditary Principalities

I shall leave aside any discussion of republics, because on another occasion I have treated them at length.[1] I will turn my attention solely to principalities and I shall proceed by weaving the threads mentioned above, discussing how these kinds of principalities may be governed and maintained.

I submit, therefore, that in hereditary states, accustomed to the rule of the bloodline of their prince, difficulties in maintaining power are considerably less than in new principalities; it is enough that the prince should not depart from the usages of his ancestors and, for the rest, to meet the needs of the times as they arise. As a result, if such a prince possesses an ordinary amount of energy, he will always maintain his position of power, unless some extraordinary and overwhelming force intervenes to take it from him. And even if he is reduced to private status, the slightest adversity which the usurper encounters, will enable him to seize possession of it again.

In Italy we have the example of the Duke of Ferrara who withstood the assaults of the Venetians in [14]84 and those of Pope Julius in [15]10 [2] for no other reason than that his family had long held power in that domain. The reason is that the natural or hereditary prince has fewer causes and less necessity to give offense. As a result, he tends to be held in greater affection, and, unless some particularly offensive characteristics of his alienate them, it stands to reason that his subjects should be well disposed to him. And in the antiquity and the continuity of the dynasty, the memories and the causes of innovations are forgotten; for one change always leaves a "toothing-stone" on which another may be built. [3]

III

Mixed Principalities

It is the new principality which is beset with difficulties. In the first place, if it is not entirely new but already formed, so that the principality to which it is added may, as a whole, be called a composite, its vicissitudes arise basically from a natural difficulty which is common to all new principalities and consists in this: that men readily change masters in the belief that they will thus better their condition. This belief leads them to take up arms against their new master, in whom they find themselves deceived, because they see that their situation has in fact been worsened. And this disillusionment arises from another natural and ordinary circumstance—the necessity which compels a new prince to offend those over whom he has recently acquired power, by the billeting of troops and by other numberless injuries which his fresh conquest draws in its train. As a result, you find that you have as enemies all those whom you have offended by occupying that new principality. Nor can you keep as your friends those who have put you in that position, because you cannot satisfy them in the way in which they had hoped to be satisfied; and also because you cannot take strong measures against them since you are in their debt. All this follows from the fact that even when one possesses complete superiority in armed forces, one still needs the collusion of some of the inhabitants in order to enter a province. For reasons such as these Louis XII, King of France, readily occupied Milan, but lost it immediately; and that first time the unaided armies of Ludovico sufficed to take it from him. For the people who

had opened its gates to him—discovering themselves
mistaken in their opinion and cheated of that future
good which they had expected to secure—found the
impositions of the new ruler intolerable.

It is very true that after rebellious regions have
been reconquered, they are lost with greater difficulty,
because the lord—taking the opportunity offered by
the rebellion—is less scrupulous or circumspect in
securing his own position. By punishing the defectors,
and ferreting out those he suspects, he strengthens his
position at the points where it is weakest. Thus, if,
the first time, all that was necessary to make France
lose Milan was a Duke Ludovico making incursions
into its confines, to make her lose it the second time
the whole world had to be arrayed against her, and
her armies had to be destroyed or expelled from
Italian soil; all of which was brought about by the
causes cited above.[4] All this notwithstanding, it *was*
taken from France both the first and the second time.
The general causes of the first loss have been discussed. It remains now to look at those of the second
and to review the remedies which were at France's
disposal and those which might be available to one
placed in that same position, which he might use to
maintain the power he had acquired and which
France *did not* use. I submit therefore that these
states which are acquired and are added to an older
dominion of the prince who acquires them are either
in the same region and have the same language or
they do not. When they are near and possess the
same language, it is a very easy matter to retain possession of them, especially when they have not been
used to living in freedom. To possess them securely,
it is enough that the line of princes which had ruled
them be eliminated; for in other matters, so long as
their old conditions are maintained and there is no

disruption of customs, men continue to live quietly. This may be illustrated from the conduct of Burgundy, Brittany, Gascony and Normandy which for so long a time have been united with France. Even though there is some difference in language, nevertheless their customs are similar and they can readily get along with each other. Anyone who acquires such domains and wants to keep them need concern himself with only two considerations: first, that the bloodline of their former rulers be extinguished; the other, that he alter neither their laws nor their taxes. In this way, in a very short time, the new and the old domains will become one body.

When, however, domains are acquired in a province which differs in language, in customs, and institutions, then difficulties arise and one has need of great good fortune and great energy to keep hold of them. And in these cases one of the greatest and most effective means is for the person who acquires them to go there to live. This action would make that possession more secure and more enduring. This is what the Turk did in Greece.[5] And in that case, notwithstanding all the other measures taken by him in order to keep possession of that state, had he not gone there to live, he would not have held it. When one is actually on the spot, disorders can be seen as they arise and remedies can be applied at once; when one is not actually present disorders are grasped only when they have become great and remedies are useless. Furthermore, the province will not be dispoiled by your officials, for the subjects find satisfaction by recourse to a prince who is at hand. This gives them greater reason to hold him in affection, if their intentions are good; if otherwise, to fear him. Anyone inclined to attack such a state from without will give great thought to the matter, so that as long as he lives there, he will lose possession of that domain only with the very greatest difficulty.

The best alternative measure is to establish colonies in one or two places, which will be, so to speak, the fetters of that state. One must either do this or keep there a large body of cavalry and infantry. Colonies involve no great expenditures. With little or no cost to himself, the prince may establish and maintain them, and in doing so he offends only those whose lands and houses he takes in order to give them to the new inhabitants, who will constitute a very small portion of that state. Those whom he does offend— since they remain poor and dispersed—can never do him any harm. The others, remaining uninjured, must of necessity be quiet for this reason and also out of fear that they might offend the prince, and bring down on themselves the same fate suffered by those who had been despoiled. I conclude therefore that these colonies cost nothing, are more loyal, and give less offense. And those who have been offended cannot return injury, since they remain, as has been remarked, dispersed and impoverished. And at this point it should be noted that men ought either to be pampered or done away with; for they take revenge for light offenses, but cannot avenge themselves for great ones. The offense, therefore, which one does to a man ought to be such that there remains no fear of revenge. If, however, instead of colonies one maintains armed forces in those domains, the cost is much greater, for all of the revenues from that state will have to be spent on the maintenance of such garrisons. The acquisition thus turns into a loss. It gives offense to many more, because it does harm to that whole state, burdening it with the billeting of an army. Everyone suffers from this burden and all therefore become his enemies. And they are enemies who can do him harm, because they remain—even though defeated—in their own homes. From every point of view, therefore, such garrisons are as useless as colonies are useful.

One who is situated in a province which differs in customs, must also, as has been said, make himself leader and defender of his less powerful neighbors, while devising every possible measure for weakening the powerful of the province. And he should be on his guard lest through some occasion some foreigner as powerful as himself gain entrance there. It will invariably happen that such an intruder will be admitted by those within the state who are dissatisfied either because they are too ambitious or because they are afraid, just as we know from history that the Aetolians thus admitted the Romans into Greece. And in every other country to which they gained entrance they were admitted by some of the inhabitants.[6] The normal course of such events is that as soon as a powerful foreigner enters a province, all of the less powerful elements in the province adhere to him, moved by the envy they feel toward their actual ruler. As a result the invader does not have to expend any energy in gaining these less powerful elements to his side because they all immediately form a unity with the power which he has acquired there. His only concern is to see to it that they do not gain too much power and too much authority. Then he can easily—through the combination of his own forces and their cooperation—bring low those who are powerful and find himself the sole arbiter of power in that province. Anyone who does not deal adroitly with these matters, will lose what he has acquired and, when he manages to keep it, will be beset by numberless difficulties and inconveniences.

The Romans observed all these precautions with

the greatest care in the provinces which they seized.
They established colonies and won over the less
powerful elements, without permitting them any real
increment of power; they brought the powerful low
and permitted no powerful foreigner to gain any
prestige within those provinces. I shall satisfy this
argument with the single example of the province of
Greece.[7] They came to terms both with the Achaeans
and the Aetolians; they destroyed the kingdom of the
Macedonians and Antiochus was driven out. They did
not permit the good services of the Aetolians and
Achaeans to bring them any increment of power. The
soft tongue of Phillip did not induce them to enter
into friendship with him before they had reduced
his power; nor, finally, could the power of Antiochus
induce them to agree to his holding any position
whatever in that province. The simple fact is that
in these instances the Romans did just what all sagacious princes must do. For such rulers must not only
look to present obstacles, but to future ones as well
and bend all their energy to obviating them. When
future ills are foreseen from a distance, they may
be readily remedied. But if you wait until they draw
near, the medicine will not be in time, for the disease
will have become incurable. As the physicians say
of a violent fever, it is easy to cure but difficult to
diagnose in its early stages; while with the passage
of time, having neither been recognized nor treated
at the beginning, it becomes easy to recognize and
difficult to cure. So it is with matters of state. The
evils which attend them can be quickly cured if they
are recognized in good time, a faculty given only to
prudent men. When, however, through not having
been recognized, they are permitted to increase to the
point where anyone can recognize them, no remedy is
any longer available.

For this reason, the Romans—since they foresaw troubles from afar—always provided against them and never permitted them to go unchecked simply to avoid war. For they knew that war is never prevented, but is simply put off to the advantage of others. They chose to make war upon Phillip and Antiochus in Greece, to forestall having to do so in Italy. At the moment, they might have avoided both the one and the other, but they did not choose to do so. Nor did they ever find satisfactory that principle which every day is heard on the lips of the wise men of our times: to take advantage of the benefit of time. They preferred to rely on their own prudence and prowess. Time carries everything before it, and can bring with it good as well as evil, evil as readily as good.

But let us turn to the example of France and let us examine whether she has done any of the things we have reviewed above. I will speak of Louis and not of Charles. Since the former held possession in Italy for a longer time, his manner of proceeding is more open to examination, and you will see that he did the contrary of those things which ought to be done in order to retain possession of a state differing in character.

King Louis found entrance into Italy through the ambition of the Venetians, who planned through his coming to gain half the territory of Lombardy for themselves. I do not wish to condemn the policy thus adopted by the king, who wished to start getting a foothold in Italy. Having no friends in this area, and finding all doors closed to him as a result of the actions of Charles, he was compelled to accept such allies as he could find. This policy would have proved well advised, had he not committed any mistakes in other affairs. By the capture of Lombardy, the king immediately regained the prestige which

Charles had lost. Genoa surrendered; the Florentines became his allies. The Marquis of Mantua, the Duke of Ferrara, the Bentivoglio, the Countess of Forlì, the Lords of Faenza, Pesaro, Rimini, Camerino, and Piombino, the citizens of Lucca, Pisa and Siena, all approached him to offer an alliance. Then finally were the Venetians able to appreciate the foolhardiness of the policy they had adopted. To acquire half of Lombardy, they had made the king lord of two thirds of Italy.

Now consider with what little difficulty the king might have retained his repute in Italy, had he observed the rules adduced above and kept all those allies of his securely dependent on himself. They were numerous, but weak and afraid, some Church men,[8] some Venetians; all, therefore, under necessity to stand by him. Through their means he would have been able to render himself secure against anyone who still retained any power. He was hardly established in Milan, however, when he did the contrary by aiding Pope Alexander to occupy the Romagna. Nor was he aware that by this decision he was weakening himself. He thus alienated his allies and those who had thrown themselves into his arms, while strengthening the Church and adding to its spiritual power, which already gave it so much authority, such vast temporal power. This first mistake made it necessary for him to commit another. To put an end to the ambition of Alexander, so that he would not become lord of Tuscany, he was compelled to come to Italy in person. It was not enough that he had made the Church great and alienated his allies; because he wanted the kingdom of Naples, he went on to divide it with the king of Spain. Thus, whereas he had, in the first place, been sole arbiter of Italy, he now shared this position with another

to whom the ambitious persons in that land and those
who were dissatisfied with his own actions, might
now have recourse: and while he might have left
in Naples a king who was his fiscal dependent, he
drove him out to install in his place another capable
of expelling him—Louis—in turn.

The desire to acquire is in truth a very natural
and ordinary thing; and when men who can, do acquire things, they will always be praised and never
condemned. When, however, they try and cannot,
and want to do so by any means whatsoever, then
they fall into error and incur condemnation. If therefore France had been able to attack Naples with her
own forces, she should have done so; if she could
not, she should not have divided it. And if it is possible to justify the division of Lombardy with the
Venetians, because it provided a foothold in Italy, the
division of Naples can only be condemned, because
no such excuse justified it.

Louis therefore had committed these five errors: he
destroyed the weaker powers; increased the power of
an agent already powerful in Italy; admitted thereto
a most powerful foreigner; failed to come to live
there; and established no colonies. And still these mistakes, while he lived, might not have injured him, had
he not commited the sixth: that of depriving the
Venetians of their power. If he had not increased the
stature of the Church, nor admitted Spain into Italy,
it would have been both politic and necessary to bring
the Venetians low. After he had committed himself to
those policies, however, he ought never to have
consented to their ruin. For as long as they were
powerful, they would always have deterred the others
from attacking Lombardy, because the Venetians
would not have permitted such an attack unless they
became lords of Lombardy by it, and because the

others would not have cared to seize it from France
only to give it to Venice. They never would have had
the courage to set upon France and Venice together.
And if someone should say that King Louis ceded the
Romagna to Alexander and the Kingdom to Spain to
avoid a war, I reply with the reasons already brought
forward above: one ought never permit a disorder to
progress to avoid war, because war is never really
avoided, but merely deferred to someone else's advantage. And if still others bring forward [as an
argument] the oath which the king had given to the
pope to undertake that campaign for him, in return
for the dissolution of his marriage and the conferring
of the cardinal's hat on Rouen, my reply will consist
in what I shall have to say further on about such
oaths given by princes and the manner in which they
are to be observed.[9]

King Louis lost Lombardy because he did not observe any of those conditions and procedures which
others who have seized provinces and wished to keep
them have observed. Nor is there any miracle involved in this, but what is most ordinary and expected. And I held a conversation about these matters at Nantes with Rouen, when Valentine (as Cesare
Borgia, the son of Pope Alexander, was popularly
called) was occupying the Romagna. When the
Cardinal of Rouen remarked to me that the Italians
did not understand war, I replied that the French
understood nothing of politics; for if they had understood anything about politics, they never would have
permitted the Church to rise to such a position of
power. And subsequent events have shown that the
power of the Church in Italy and of Spain has been
brought about by France, while its own ruin has been
brought about by them. From all this a general rule
may be deduced, which rarely, if ever, fails: he who

brings another to power prepares his own ruin. For that power is created by him either by device or by force. And the man who becomes powerful is rightly suspicious of both the one and the other.

IV

Why the Kingdom of Darius, Which Alexander Had Occupied, Did Not Rebel Against the Successors of Alexander After His Death

After considering the difficulties involved in keeping a state which has been acquired for the first time, someone might well wonder how it could come about that Alexander the Great became Lord of Asia in a few years and, almost immediately after occupying it, died. Under these circumstances it would seem to be expected that that entire state would have risen up in rebellion. Nevertheless, his successors kept control of it and in the process encountered only those difficulties which arose among themselves as a consequence of their own ambitions.[10] My answer is that all principalities, of which we have record, are found to have been governed in two different ways: either by a single prince, to whom all others are absolutely subject and who take part in the government of that realm only as his ministers by his grace and concession; or by a prince and barons together. The latter hold their position not by the grace of the lord, but by antiquity of blood descent. Such barons have territories and subjects of their own, who recognize their lordship and entertain a natural attachment for them. Those provinces which are governed by a single prince and his dependent agents, hold their lord in greater authority, for in all that territory no one but he is recognized as having supreme power. If they obey any one else, they do so in his character as minister and official and bear him no particular affection. The two examples of this difference in government in our own times are the Turk and the King of France. The entire monarchy of the Turk is governed by a single lord, and all others are merely his agents. His realm is divided into satrapies; he sends different administrators into them and changes and varies these administrators as seems good to him. The King of France, by contrast, finds himself surrounded by a large number of lords of ancient descent, recognized by their own subjects and held in affection by them. They have their own pre-eminence; nor may the king, without danger to himself, infringe upon it. Considering, therefore, the one and the other of these states, one will find that great difficulty would attend the conquest of the Turkish monarchy. But once conquered, it could be held with little difficulty. The reason why the realm of the Turk must prove so difficult to seize arises from the fact that the prospective invader cannot be invited in by the princes of that realm. Nor can he hope through the rebellion of those about the Turk to facilitate his own undertaking; and all of this follows from the reasons adduced above. Since they are all slaves and under direct obligation, they are more difficult to corrupt. When they are corrupted, little help can be looked for from them, since they command no following among the people; also for reasons noted above. Whoever undertakes to attack the Turkish realm must therefore expect to find it entirely united and he had better place his hopes more on his own forces than on disorders within, instigated by others. Once the Turk is conquered, however, and so broken in the

field that he cannot regroup his forces, thought need
be given only to the bloodline of the prince. Once
this is wiped out, there is no one else whom one
need fear, for the others have no repute among the
people. Before his victory the victor could place no
hope in them; so, afterward, he has no reason to
fear them.

The contrary holds true in realms governed as is
that of France. It is easy to enter them by winning
to one's side some baron of the realm; for malcontents are always to be found as well as those eager
for innovations. These, for reasons already noted,
can open to you the way to that state and make
victory easier for you. To maintain that victory thereafter, however, entails innumerable difficulties, involv-
ing both those who have aided you and those whom
you have oppressed. It will not suffice simply to
extinguish the bloodline of that prince. There remain those lords, who make themselves the leaders
of new changes. And since you can neither satisfy
nor obliterate them, you lose that state, on the first
occassion.

Now if you will consider of which nature the government of Darius partook, you will find that it was
like that of the Turk. For this reason, Alexander
had first to defeat him as a united force and drive
him from the countryside.[11] After that victory, and
with the death of Darius, Alexander remained in
secure possession of that state, for the reasons which
have been discussed above. And his successors—had
they remained united—might have enjoyed it at
their ease. As a matter of fact, in that realm no
other troubles arose than those which they themselves incited. But states organized like that of
France are impossible to hold with such great security. Hence arose the frequent rebellions in Spain,

France and Greece, against the Romans, because
those realms were composed of many subordinate
states. As a consequence, for so long as the memory
of those states persisted, the Romans always remained
uncertain of their possession. However, once that
memory was extinguished—through the might and
the daily presence of the imperial power—the Romans became secure possessors of those regions. And
even the Romans, when civil war arose among them,
were severally able to draw after themselves a part
of those provinces, according to the authority which
each rival had established in them.[12] And those provinces recognized only the Romans because the blood-
lines of their ancient lords had been extinguished.
One who reflects on these events will not wonder at
the ease with which Alexander kept possession of
Asia, nor at the difficulties which others, such as
Pyrrhus, encountered in conserving what they
had conquered. The contrast does not arise from the
greater or lesser capacity of the conqueror, but from
the difference between the lands they conquered.

N. B.

v

*How to Govern Cities or Principalities
Which, Before They Were Occupied, Were
Living Under Their Own Laws*

When those states which have been acquired, as
has been said, are accustomed to living under their
own laws and in freedom, there are three ways to
keep them in subjection: first, destroy them; second,
take up personal residence in them; third, permit them
to go on living under their own laws, meanwhile
drawing tribute from them and creating within them

a ruling minority which will see to it that those laws remain favorable to you. Since that ruling minority, or oligarchy, has been created by the prince, it knows that it cannot endure without his power and friendship and must do everything to maintain him in power. And it is much easier, when one wishes to preserve it, to rule such a city used to living in freedom, by means of its own citizens, than in any other manner.

The Spartans and the Romans are examples. Sparta held Athens and Thebes by creating such minorities within them; nevertheless, they lost them. The Romans, to hold Capua, Carthage and Numantia, destroyed but did not lose them. They wanted to hold Greece just as the Spartans had, making it free and leaving it its own laws, but were not successful in this. Instead, they were forced to destroy many cities of that province to hold it. For, as a matter of fact, there is no sure way of holding them except by destroying them. Anyone who becomes master of a city accustomed to its freedom and does not destroy it, may expect to be destroyed by it. For that city can always use the name of freedom and its ancient institutions as a shield for rebellion. For these [freedoms] are never forgotten, despite the passage of time and benefits conferred. And no matter what steps are taken or provisions made, that name and those institutions are never forgotten unless the inhabitants are disunited and scattered. On the contrary, immediate recourse is had to them in every incident, as happened in Pisa a hundred years after it had been subjected by the Florentines. But when cities or provinces are accustomed to live under a prince and that bloodline is extinguished, they are slower to take up arms. On the one hand, they are accustomed to obey; while, on the other, deprived of their old ruler, they cannot come to any agreement among themselves on the choice of a new one from their own number nor do they know how to live in freedom. As a result, a prince can readily win them and secure control of them. In republics, however, there is greater vitality, hatred, and desire for revenge. The memory of that former freedom neither is, nor can be, permitted to lie quiescent. As a result, the safer way is either to raze them or to take up residence in them.

VI

New Principalities Which Are Acquired by One's Own Arms and Prowess

No one should be astonished if, in the remarks which I shall make concerning entirely new principalities, both with regard to the ruler and with regard to organization, I use examples of the very great. Since men almost always walk in paths which have already been trodden by others and base their actions on imitation of others—even though they can neither entirely hold to the paths of their models nor attain their stature—it behooves a prudent man always to take the path trodden by great men and to imitate those who have been most outstanding, so that though his own achievement may not equal theirs, it may at least exude some fragrance of the same greatness. He should do as experienced bowmen do. When the place they want to hit seems to them too far away, knowing how far their arrows will carry, they sight their aim much higher than the destined target—not that they can attain that height with their arrows, but that they may reach the target they have in mind with the help of this higher aim. I submit therefore that in entirely new principalities, where there is a new prince, greater or less difficulty will be encountered in maintaining them as the one who has conquered them is more or less accomplished and resourceful. And since this achievement, of passing from the status of private person to that of ruling prince, presupposes either fortune or capacity, it would seem that one or the other of these will mitigate in part many of his difficulties. Nevertheless, the man who has relied less on fortune, has maintained his position more effectively. This is rendered still easier if the prince is compelled to take up personal residence there, because he has no other possessions.

To mention those who by their own capacities and not by fortune have become ruling princes, I submit that the most outstanding are Moses, Cyrus, Romulus, Theseus and others like them.[13] Although we ought not really to discuss Moses since he was the mere agent of things which were commissioned him by God, still he is to be admired if only for that quality of person which made him worthy to speak with God. When we consider Cyrus and the others who have established or conquered states, you will find them all worthy of admiration. And if we proceed to the examination of their particular actions and institutions, they will appear in no way inferior to those of Moses, though he had so great a teacher. The examination of their actions and their lives shows that they had no other fortune than the opportunity or occasion which furnished them with the matter into which they could introduce the form which they deemed right. Without that opportunity, their resourcefulness would have been wasted. Lacking that capacity, the opportunity would have presented itself

in vain. It was therefore necessary that Moses should
find the people of Israel in Egypt, enslaved and oppressed by the Egyptians, so that they might be disposed to follow him to escape from their servitude. It
was necessary that Romulus should not have remained in Alba and have been exposed at birth so
that he might become King of Rome and the founder
of that nation. It was necessary that Cyrus should
find the Persians restive under the Median power and
the Medes grown soft and effeminate as the result
of a long period of peace. Nor would Theseus have
been able to demonstrate his resourcefulness, if he
had not found the Athenians dispersed. These opportunities, therefore, made these men successful,
while their exceptional capacities enabled them to
recognize the opportunity as it arose. By this combination their fatherlands were ennobled and rose
to heights of prosperity.

There were those who, like these men, became
ruling princes because of their native ability, seizing
their principalities with difficulty but holding them
with ease. The difficulties which they encountered in
the acquisition of their power arose in part from
the novel procedures and arrangements which they
were forced to introduce in order to establish their
power and to make secure the possession of it. One
should reflect seriously that there is nothing more difficult to accomplish, nor more dubious in its outcome, nor more perilous in its execution than to
take the initiative in introducing new institutions. For
the innovator has as his enemies all those who prof-
ited from the old arrangements and he has only half-
hearted defenders in all those who stand to gain by
the new. The tepidity of the latter arises in part from
fear of their adversaries who have the laws on their
side, in part from the native incredulity of men. For

men never actually believe in anything new, until they have had some reassuring experience of it. Whence it happens that whenever those who are unfavorable to the changes have an opportunity of attacking them, they do so with partisan zeal, while those others offer only lukewarm defense; thus the innovator finds himself endangered from both sides.

Since we wish to discuss this question thoroughly, we must go on to ask whether these innovators are self-sufficient or whether they depend on others; that is, whether, to achieve their purposes, they must ask help of others or whether they can carry them through on their own resources. In the first case, they inevitably end up badly and bring nothing to a successful termination. When, however, they rely on their own resources and can carry through their purposes with these, then rarely do they fall into danger. This is the reason why all of the armed prophets have been victorious, while the unarmed have perished. In addition to what has been said, the nature of peoples is fickle. While it is easy to persuade them, it is difficult to make them stand firm in any persuasion. Therefore, affairs must be so ordered that when they no longer believe, it is possible to make them believe by force. Moses, Cyrus, Theseus and Romulus never would have been able to assure the observation of the political order they established for any length of time, had they been unarmed. The experience of Fra Girolamo Savonarola, in our own times, points this up. He met disaster in his innovations when the multitude ceased to believe in him; he lacked the means of making believers stand fast and to force the unbelieving to believe. Such men, therefore, have great difficulty in carrying through their designs. All their dangers lie in the effort, so that they must overcome those dangers by their own powers. However, once these dangers have been overcome, and when they have begun to be held in veneration—and those who might have nursed envy of their capacity have been exterminated—they remain powerful, secure, honored, blessed among men.

To these important examples, I should like to add a lesser one, which, however, exhibits a certain proportion to them and which I would like to have stand for all other similar examples: Hiero of Syracuse. This man, from the position of a private citizen, went on to become ruler of Syracuse. Fortune furnished him nothing but the opportunity. When the Syracusans were oppressed, they chose him as their military leader. From this position he earned the right to be their ruling prince. He was a man of such immense capacity, even in the conduct of his private affairs, that the historian[14] who writes of him says:

"quod nihil illi deerat ad regnandum praeter regnum," "no quality of a ruler was lacking to him except a kingdom."

He dissolved the old form of military organization, and formed a new one; he set aside old friendships to make new ones. When he had alliances and soldiers which were his own, he could on this foundation build as he chose. What cost him great effort to acquire, cost him little to maintain.

VII

New Principalities Acquired by the Armed Forces of Others and by Fortune

Those who exchange the state of private citizen for that of ruler solely by fortune effect this change with ease but maintain their new status with considerable trouble. They encounter no difficulties in the process, because they fly along the path to power. All their woes arise after they have attained their new position. Such are those to whom political power comes by purchase or through the favor of another who grants it to him. This was the case with many rulers in Greece, Ionia and along the Hellespont, who were made satraps by Darius with the understanding that they would hold those places for his security and glory. This was also the case with those Roman commanders who, starting as private persons, reached the imperial power by bribing soldiers. Such rulers are wholly dependent on the goodwill and the favor of the one who has conceded power to them, two most unstable and insecure foundations. They neither know how to maintain their position, nor have they the power to do so. They don't know how to. Because if a man has always lived as a private person, it is not reasonable to expect him to know how to command. Nor are they able [commanders], because they have no forces loyal and devoted to them. Furthermore, states which come into being suddenly, like all things in nature which are born and grow swiftly, sink such [shallow] roots and branches that the first spell of bad weather uproots them. Those men who, as has been stated, come suddenly to power without preparation [will not succeed], unless they are of such innate capacity that they know immediately how to go about preparing themselves to conserve what fortune has placed in their laps, laying down such foundations afterwards as others would have already established before becoming rulers.

I would like to cite two examples which illustrate respectively the two methods of acquiring ruling status, by personal capacity or by fortune, namely, Francesco Sforza and Cesare Borgia, both within the memory of living men. Francesco, through the correct measures and by the exercise of his great personal capabilities, rose from private estate to become Duke of Milan. And the position which he achieved by a thousand struggles, he maintained with little effort. By contrast, Cesare Borgia, commonly known as the Duke of Valentino, gained his position of power through the favor of his father and lost it when that favor failed; and this despite the fact that he used every means and did everything that a prudent and resourceful man should do to send down strong roots in those positions of power which the favor and the armed assistance of others had brought to him. For, as has been noted above, one who has not laid down the foundations of power before acceding to it, can indeed still do so after acquiring it, through the requisite personal capacity, though with great trouble to the architect and danger to the structure. Indeed, if one considers all the steps the Duke had taken, it would be seen that he had as a matter of fact established solid foundations for future exercise of power. And I think it well worth while to dwell upon these measures, because I would not know what better precepts to suggest to a new prince than the example of his actions. If the arrangements which he had made came finally to naught, it was through no fault of his, but through an extreme and extraordinary malice of fortune.

Alexander VI, in his plans to make a great and potent prince of the Duke, his son, faced a great number of obstacles both immediate and future. In the first place, he did not see any way in which he might make the Duke sovereign of a state which was not a state of the Church. Further, should he to this end wish to detach some state from the possessions of the Church, he knew that the Duke of Milan and the Venetians would not give their consent to such an expedient, because Faenza and Rimini were already under the protection of the Venetian. He saw, furthermore, that the armed forces of Italy and especially those of which he might have made use, were under the control of persons who had reason to be fearful of the aggrandizement of the Pope. He could therefore place no confidence in those forces since they were all in the hands of the Orsini, the Colonna, and their adherents. It was therefore necessary to upset those prevailing arrangements—to bring disorder into the spheres of power of these groups—in order to secure mastery of some part of their possessions. This proved easy of accomplishment, because he found that the Venetians, for other reasons, had resolved to give the French fresh access into Italy, a movement which he not only did not impede, but which he actually rendered easier by dissolving the earlier marriage of King Louis. The King therefore re-entered Italy with the aid of the Venetians and with the consent of [Pope] Alexander. No sooner was the King established in Milan than the Pope secured from him forces for the undertaking against the Romagna; this region was conceded to him in virtue of the reputation which the King enjoyed in Italy.

Having seized the Romagna and unseated the Colonna, the Duke found his plans to consolidate this acquisition and to advance his projects impeded by two obstacles: the first, his own troops which did not seem to him to be loyal or trustworthy; the second, the designs of France. That is, he feared that the troops of the Orsini, of which he had made use, would withdraw their support, not only impeding further acquisitions, but taking from him what he had already secured, and that the King, in his turn, might do the same. He had an intimation of this in regard to the Orsini when, after the capture of Faenza, he assaulted Bologna; for he saw that they lacked all enthusiasm in the latter undertaking. He gained a similar insight into the mind of the King after the capture of the dukedom of Urbino. The Duke then turned his forces against Tuscany, but the King made him desist from this attack. As a consequence the Duke came to the decision to rely no more upon the forces and the favor of others. As a first step in this direction, he set out to weaken the parties of the Orsini and the Colonna in Rome. He did this by showering on the high-born adherents of those factions great largesse, appointing them to posts of leadership and government commensurate with the honor due their station. As a consequence, within a few months, all partisan attachment had been extinguished in them and they all gave their allegiance to the Duke. His next step was to wait for an opportunity of destroying the leaders of the Orsini faction, having already scattered those of the house of Colonna. The desired occasion soon presented itself and he made the most of it. The Orsini, realizing somewhat tardily that the aggrandizement of the Duke and of the Church spelled their own ruin, summoned a conference at Magione near Perugia.[15] From this conference were born the rebellion in Urbini and the uprisings in the Romagna and numberless other dangers to the position of the Duke, all of which he overcame with the help of the French. Having in this way re-established his reputation, and placing his faith no longer either in the French or in any other external forces— for fear of placing himself in their power—he turned to deceptions. He knew so well how to dissimulate his own intentions that the Orsini, through the offices of Prince Paolo, established relations with him. The Duke neglected no ruse of diplomacy to reassure Prince Paolo, showering him with gifts of money, clothing and horses. As a result, the simplicity of the Orsini led them to Sinigaglia into the hands of the Duke. With the loss of their leaders and the conversion of their partisans to his own cause, the Duke had laid the foundations of his power well; for he possessed the whole of the Romagna together with the duchy of Urbino. And, greatest advantage of all, those peoples now seemed genuinely devoted to him because they had begun to experience a heightened prosperity under his rule.

Because this matter of the Romagna is most noteworthy and its conduct deserves to be imitated by others, I will venture to dwell on it somewhat at length. After the Duke had taken possession of the Romagna, he found that it had been controlled by ruthless noblemen, more alert to despoil their subjects than to rule them well. Thus they had created anarchy rather than union among them to the extent that that province was filled with thieves and brigands and every other kind of disregard for law. The Duke therefore decided that in order to reduce the province to a state of peace and obedience to the royal arm he must give it a good government. To this end he installed as governor Ramiro de Orco, a ruthless and efficient man, bestowing complete power upon him. This man quickly reduced that province to a state of peace and unity, gaining a considerable reputation for himself while doing so. Thereupon the Duke decided that such excessive authority was not necessary, fearing that it might become hateful. He therefore established a civil tribunal in the center of the province, presided over by a man of excellent parts, before which each city of the province had its repre-

sentative. Because he knew that the rigorous measures exercised in the past had generated some hatred
toward himself, he wished to remove this sentiment
from the minds of those people and win them entirely to himself, by showing them that those measures had been due not to any order of his but to the
harsh character of his minister. Seizing this opportunity, he caused the body of Ramiro to be found
cut in two one morning in the piazza at Cesana, with
a piece of wood and a bloody knife beside it. The
savagery of that spectacle left the people in a state
of combined satisfaction and stupification.

But let us now return to the point at which we
digressed. The Duke, I say, now found himself quite
powerful and relatively secure from imminent dangers
because he now possessed troops of his own and because he had, for the most part, destroyed the neighboring forces which might have done him harm. In
order to press his acquisitions, however, he found
that he would have to proceed with circumspection
where the King of France was concerned, for he
knew that the King—who somewhat tardily had come
to realize his mistake—would not support him. Consequently, he began to seek out new alliances and to
temporize with France concerning the campaign
which the French were mounting against the Spaniards who had been laying seige to Gaeta. His intention was to gain some pledge of Spanish support,
which he would have gotten, had [Pope] Alexander
lived.[16]

These were the dispositions he made concerning
present issues. As far as future developments were
concerned, his chief worry was that a new successor
in the Church would not be favorably disposed toward him and might seek to wrest from him what
[Pope] Alexander had given him. Against such a de-

velopment, he thought he could provide in four ways:
first, by killing all of the blood-relations of the rulers
whom he had despoiled, to deprive a new and hostile
pope of any possible support from that quarter;
second, by gaining to his own allegience all the noblemen of Rome, as we have noted, in order by their
means to keep the Pope in check; third, to bind the
College of Cardinals as closely to himself as possible; fourth, to gain so much control, before the
Pope should die, that completely through his own resources he could resist any first onslaught against him.

Of these four proposals, he had achieved three by
the time [Pope] Alexander died; the fourth had almost been brought to a successful conclusion. Of the
lords whom he had despoiled he had killed as many
as he could lay hands on, and very few escaped
him; he had gained the Roman patricians to his
party and had a large majority of the College of
Cardinals on his side. As for new conquests, he had
laid plans to become Lord of Tuscany; he already
possessed Perugia and Piombino and he had taken
Pisa under his protection. And since he no longer
had to go cautiously where France was concerned—
for France had already been despoiled of the Kingdom of Naples by the Spaniards, with the result that
both of those parties were under the necessity of
seeking to purchase his friendship—he seized complete control of Pisa. After this, Lucca and Siena immediately surrendered, partly out of jealousy toward
the Florentines and partly out of fear. The Florentines had no alternative except to surrender in turn.
And if that had gone well—as indeed it was going
well the year that [Pope] Alexander died—he would
have acquired so much power and such reputation that
he would have been henceforth entirely his own master, dependent no longer on the support and favor of

others, but solely on his own. But [Pope] Alexander died only five years after Cesare Borgia had first drawn his sword. That death left him with only the realm of the Romagna solidly established and with all his other projects up in the air, caught between two very powerful enemy armies and himself sick unto death.

And still there was in the Duke such fierceness of purpose and such resourcefulness—so well did he understand how the allegiance of men is to be won and lost, and so solid were the foundations of power which he had laid down in such a short time—that if he had not had those armies on his back and if he had been in good health, he still would have won out over every obstacle. And that the foundations he had cast were indeed solid is to be seen from the fact that even then the Romagna waited for him for more than a month. In Rome, though only half alive, he held his ground; and although the Baglioni, the Vitelli and the Orsini had entered Rome they could find no one whom they might lead against him. He still had the power to see to it that the new pope would be, if not precisely the man he wanted, at least no one whom he did not wish to see in that position. If at the death of [Pope] Alexander, Cesare had himself been in good health, everything would still have been easy for him. And he told me, on the day on which Julius II was made pope, that he had given thought to everything that might happen on the death of his father and that he had made provision against every eventuality. But he had never thought that on his father's death, he would himself be at death's door.

Having thus reviewed all the actions of the Duke, I could find no ground on which to censure him; rather it seemed to me that I ought, as I have done, propose him as an example to be imitated by all those who have come to positions of political power through the arms and the favor of others. For being a man of great spirit and soaring ambitions, he could not have conducted himself in any other way. Only the brevity of [Pope] Alexander's life and his own illness put an end to his designs. Whoever, therefore, in his new principality thinks it necessary to secure himself against his enemies, to gain allies, to win out whether by force or fraud, to make himself beloved or feared by the people, followed and revered by his soldiers, to destroy those who can or have reason to do you harm, to reorganize ancient institutions, to be severe and still acceptable, magnanimous and liberal, to destroy the older military establishment and set up a new one, maintain alliances with kings and princes, in such a way that they must do you favors with graciousness or move circumspectly against you, can find no more impressive examples than the actions of this man. The only error which can be alleged against him is the creation of Julius II [as pope], for in this he made a bad choice. Since, as had been noted, he could not choose the pope he wished—he could still have prevented anyone unwanted by him from becoming pope—he should never have acceded to the creation as pope of one of those cardinals whom he had offended or who, on becoming pope, might entertain any fear of him. For men strike out either through fear or hatred. Those whom he had injured were, among others, San Pietro ad Vincula, Colonna, San Giorgio and Ascanio. All the others, had they been elected, would have had reason to be afraid of him, except Rouen and the Spaniards. The Spaniards were his fellow-countrymen and thus under obligation to him; Rouen had nothing to fear because he had the support of France. Therefore the Duke, before all else, should have seen to it that a

Spaniard was created pope; failing this, he should
have supported Rouen and not San Pietro ad Vincula.
For anyone who thinks that among great personages
new benefits obliterate the memory of old offenses,
deludes himself. The Duke, therefore, made a mistake in this election and this was the final reason or
cause of his downfall.

VIII

Those Who Come to Political Power Through Crime

Since there are still two ways of passing from
private status to that of prince which cannot entirely
be attributed either to fortune or personal capacity, it
seems to me that they ought not to be passed over
here, even though one of them might be treated more
elaborately in a discussion of republics. The first of
these is to ascend to a position of ruling power
through some crime or nefarious deed; the second is
the elevation of a private citizen to the position of
prince of his country through the favour of his fellow citizens. The first of these two ways may be
illustrated by two examples, the one from ancient
times, the other modern. And in introducing these
examples, I shall not debate the merits of the subject, because I think that the examples themselves
will be enough for anyone who feels that he must
imitate them.

Agathocles, the Sicilian,[17] rose to be king of Syracuse, not merely from the status of private citizen
but from the most abject social station. This man,
the son of a potter, rose through every stage of his
career by crime. Nevertheless, in the perpetration of

his crimes he displayed such physical prowess and resourcefulness of spirit that upon joining the military forces, he rose through its grades to become praetor of Syracuse. Having become established in that position, he formed the determination to become ruler and to hold by violence and without obligation to others that which had been granted him by common consent; and he reached an understanding concerning this design with Hamilcar, the Carthaginian, campaigning with his forces at that time in Sicily. One morning he called together the Senate and the people of Syracuse, as though to discuss with them matters of the public interest. But upon a prearranged sign, his soldiers fell upon and slew all the Senators and the richest citizens. With these disposed of, he seized control of that city and held it without any sign of civil protest. And even though he was twice defeated by the Carthaginians and the city was finally subjected to seige, he was not only able to defend the city but also—leaving a part of his forces behind to defend it—to carry the attack into Africa. In a short time he had relieved the seige of the city and had reduced the Carthaginians to such straits that they had to reach an agreement with him, according to the terms of which they retired to Africa leaving Sicily uncontested to Agathocles. Anyone who considers the actions and the resourcefulness of that man will find little if anything to attribute to fortune—in as much as he reached his position of power not by anyone's favor, but through the grades of the military organization, with a thousand dangers and labours to himself and thereafter held on to it by so many dangerous and bold expedients. Still, one cannot call it character to kill one's fellow-citizens, betray friends, disavow oaths, and lack reverence and religion; such actions can gain one possession of power, but not renown. As a matter of fact, when one reflects on Agathocles' courage and resourcefulness in confronting and escaping unscathed from perils, and his steadfastness of will in bearing and overcoming adverse circumstances, there is no reason to consider him inferior in any of these respects to other widely renowned captains. Nevertheless, his cruelty and inhumanity, displayed in his countless crimes, do not permit him to be celebrated among men of outstanding character. Therefore, one cannot attribute either to fortune or personal capacity what he achieved without the one or the other.

In our own times, during the reign of [Pope] Alexander VI, we encounter Oliverotto of Fermo. Left an orphan at an early age, he was raised by a maternal uncle, Giovanni Fogliani by name. In his early manhood he entered military service under Paolo Vitelli and, excelling in that discipline, quickly reached a high post of military authority. After the death of Paolo, he campaigned under Vitellozzo, Paolo's brother. And in a very short time, by his resourcefulness, vigor of mind and body, and personal bearing, rose to be second in command of that military organization.

It seemed to him, however, a poor estate, to remain in the service of others. Therefore, with the collusion of certain citizens of Fermo to whom slavery was more precious than the freedom of their country, and with the connivance of Vitellozzo, he devised a plan to seize Fermo. He therefore wrote to Giovanni Fogliani, protesting that since he had been away from home for some years he would like to come to visit him, and at the same time look into certain affairs pertaining to his inheritance. Moreover, he went on to say, since he had expended himself during those years only in quest of honor, he would like his fellow citizens to see that they had not been spent in vain; he wanted therefore to come home in fitting style accompanied by a hundred horsemen from among his companions and retainers. He begged his uncle to see to it that they would all be received by the citizens of Fermo with due honor. He closed by pointing out that all this would honor not only himself, Oliverotto, but also Fogliani, as the man who had raised him. Giovanni did not fail his nephew in any respect in all the arrangements for his honorable reception; he not only saw to it that he was received with acclaim by the citizens of Fermo, but also lodged him in his own house. After some days, Oliverotto, having completed all the arrangements necessary for the crime he was contemplating, gave a solemn and elaborate banquet to which he invited Giovanni Fogliani and all of the first citizens of Fermo. When they had regaled themselves and enjoyed the entertainment which usually accompanies such feasts, Oliverotto designedly began to raise some serious discussions, speaking of the greatness of Pope Alexander and of Cesare Borgia, his son, and of their enterprises. Giovanni and the others replied in kind to these remarks, whereupon Oliverotto arose in feigned anger, protesting that these were matters which ought to be discussed only in more secluded places. With that, he withdrew into another apartment and Giovanni and all of the others followed him. No sooner had they seated themselves anew than from their hiding places in the apartment soldiers sprang out and slaughtered Giovanni and all the rest.

After this massacre, Oliverotto mounted his horse and rode through the town laying siege with his men to the supreme council of magistrates in its official palace. Terrified, its members consented to

his demand to establish a new government with
him as its head. He proceeded to consolidate his new
position by putting to death all the malcontents who
might cause him any trouble and by establishing new
military and civil ordinances. And he did these things
so expeditiously that within the space of the year
in which he held that position of power, he was not
only unchallenged in Fermo but had in addition become an object of fear to all the neighboring cities.
And his removal from this position would have been
as difficult as that of Agathocles had he not permitted
himself to be ensnared by Cesare Borgia, when the
latter, as we have already narrated, seized the Orsini
and the Vitelli at Sinigaglia. For Oliverotto also was
lured there, a year after his parricide, and strangled
together with Vitellozzo who had been his master
alike in boldness and crime.

Some might doubt that it could come about that
an Agathocles, or anyone like him, after numberless
cruelties and betrayals, could live for a long time secure in his own city, could defend it from its external
enemies and never become the object of a conspiracy
among its citizens, while others, through similar
cruelties, have not been able to keep control of a
state even in peaceful times to say nothing of times
of troubles and war. I believe that the difference lies
in the good and the bad uses of harshness. Those
cruelties may be called well-used—if one can apply
the term good to evils—which are committed at one
stroke to make one's own position secure, and which
are not then persisted in; but, on the contrary, are
then converted to the utility of the subjects whenever possible. By contrast, those are ill-used which,
though in the beginning were few, tend rather to increase with time than to diminish or disappear. Those
who proceed in the first manner can, through some

compact with God and men, secure their possession of political power as Agathocles did; but it is impossible that those who proceed in the second manner should maintain their position. All of which leads us to the observation that in seizing a state, the usurper should review all the injuries which it will be necessary for him to commit, and commit them all at once so that he will not have to renew them daily. Thus by not having to renew them he can reassure men and win them over to himself by means of benefits conferred upon them. He who does otherwise, whether through timidity or through bad advice, must forever go about knife in hand and can never establish his authority over his subjects; for these will never have confidence in him because of his renewed assaults upon them. Injuries being distasteful ought all to be done at one time, so that they offend the less; benefits, by contrast, ought to be doled out a little at a time, so that their good taste may linger. Above all, a prince should live with his subjects in such a manner that no incident, good or bad, should cause him to alter his course of action. For when adverse times bring with them the necessity for severe measures, these are no longer timely and do not serve. And the good that you do, under pressure of necessity, does you no credit, because people know that it has been forced from you and give you no thanks for it.

IX

The Civil Principality

We come now to that other instance in which a private citizen becomes prince of his native city, not by any crime or other intolerable act of violence, but through the consent of his other fellow citizens. This we may call a civil principality. To arrive at such a position a man needs neither personal capacity alone nor fortune alone, but rather a certain astuteness favored by fortune. I submit that one arrives at such a position of ruling power either by the favor of the people or by that of the nobles. In every city there is present the tendency to form these two diverse classes. As a consequence, the people desire not to be commanded nor oppressed by the nobles, while the nobles desire both to command and to oppress the people. These diverse movements give rise in every city to one or another of three possible states of affairs: a principality, liberty, or anarchy.

The principality is created either by the people or by the nobles, according as one or the other of these parties is given an opportunity. When the nobles realize that they cannot impose their will upon the people, they begin to build up the reputation of one of their own number and elect him prince, so that in his shadow they may achieve their purposes. The people in its turn, seeing that it cannot effectively resist the nobles, do the same with one of themselves and make him prince so that in his authority they may find their own defense. The man who comes to a position of power through the help of the nobles maintains his position with greater difficulty than one who attains it with the help of the people. He finds himself surrounded by many who consider themselves his equals; as a result he cannot command or manipulate them as he might wish. The man who attains power by the favor of the people, by contrast, finds himself alone in that position with no one, or very few, about him who are not prepared to obey him. Furthermore, it is not possible for a prince to satisfy the desires of the nobles honestly and without injury to others; but this is possible with the people. The purposes of the people are more honest than those of the nobles; for the latter want to oppress others, while the desire of the former is simply not to be oppressed. Moreover, a prince can never make himself wholly secure against a people which is hostile to him, for they are too many. He can, however, secure himself against the nobles, because they are few in number. The worst that a prince can expect from a hostile populace is to be abandoned by it. If the nobles are his enemies, he must fear not only abandonment but that they may actually set upon him. For the nobles have more perception and astuteness in these matters; they always take timely action in their own interests and they try to establish obligations toward themselves in those whom they hope will win out. Furthermore, it is necessary for the prince always to live with that same populace; but he can fare well enough without those same nobles, for he can make and break, give and take away their standing from day to day.

To bring greater light to this matter, I would point out that the nobles must be considered principally in two ways. Either they conduct themselves in such a manner that by their way of life they become wholly dependent upon your own fortunes, or they do not. Those who do become dependent in this fashion and are not rapacious, should be honored and held in esteem; those who do not do so, must be examined from two points of view. They may act in this manner through cowardice or natural lack of spirit. When this is the case, you should make use of them, especially those who can give you sound counsel. For in prosperous times they will honor you, while in adverse times you have nothing to fear from them. On the other hand, they may remain independent of you deliberately with a view to their own ambitions; when this is the case, it is a sign that they are more concerned with themselves than with you. Against such as these, the prince must be on his guard, fearing them as he would his avowed enemies; for invariably, in times of trouble, they will help bring you to ruin.

A man who has become prince through the favor of the people ought to maintain their allegiance. This should be easy for him, since all they demand is freedom from oppression. However, the man, who, contrary to the disposition of the people, becomes prince through the favor of the nobles, must, before all else, seek to win the people over to himself; this too will prove easy if he will but take them under his protection. And because men who receive good at the hands of one from whom they had expected evil, become more obligated to their benefactor, the people will immediately become more favorably disposed toward him than they would have been had he been elevated to his position through their own favor. There are, moreover, many ways in which the prince can win the people over to himself, which, because of their great variety, cannot readily be reduced to certain rules. For this reason we will discuss them no further. I shall only conclude that a prince must have the people favorably disposed to him; otherwise he has no recourse in adversities.

Nabis, prince of the Spartans, withstood a siege by the whole of Greece and by a victorious Roman army, defending against them both his country and his own personal power; and all he had to do, when danger overtook him, was to secure his position against a few persons. Clearly, this would not have been enough had he had the people against him. And let no one oppose my opinion with that trite proverb that "he who builds upon the people, builds upon mud." That saying is true when a private citizen makes the people the basis of his power, persuading himself that the people will free him when he shall be oppressed by his enemies or by magistrates. In such case, one may frequently find onself deceived, as the Gracchi did in Rome and Giorgio Scali in Florence. But when it is a prince who bases his power on the people—one who knows how to command and who is a man of courage, who does not buckle under adversities and takes all due precautions, who keeps the entire populace encouraged by his own spirit and by the institutions he sets up—never will such a man find himself deceived by them and he will be found to have sunk his foundations well.

This type of principality is subject to danger, when it is about to pass from civil status to one of absolute power. Princes who take this step of assuming absolute power, rule either in their own persons or through officials. In the latter case, their position is weaker and in greater danger, because they must rely completely upon the will of the persons who have been named to office; for the latter, especially in adverse times, can take their position away from them with great facility, either by rising against them or by refusing to obey them. And when dangers are upon him, the prince is not in time to seize absolute power; for the citizens and subjects, who are accustomed to receiving their commands from the magistrates are not disposed, in such moments of peril, to accept his [rule]. And he will always find, in adverse times, a dearth of those in whom he can put his trust. Such a prince cannot predicate his position on the experience of quiet times, when the citizens have no need of his power. During such times when death seems far away, every one runs at his word and everyone is ready to die for him. In adverse times, however, when the state power has need of its citizens, then there are few to be found on whom to rely. Such an experience is all the more dangerous because one can undergo it only once. The wise prince must therefore devise a form of government under which his citizens are at all times and in every variety of circumstances in need of his ruling power. Only then will they prove constantly faithful to him.

Bases for faithfulness

X

How the Powers of All Principalities Are to Be Measured

It is wise to include in the examination of the characteristics of these principalities another consideration, namely, whether the prince has such a position of power that he can, in case of necessity, maintain that position entirely on his own resources or whether he must always call upon others to defend him. The better to clarify this theme, I submit the opinion that those princes can maintain themselves who have adequate manpower or sufficient money to organize an army able to take the field against anyone who might venture to attack them. In like fashion, I believe that these must always have recourse to others who cannot take the field against an enemy but must take refuge behind their walls and remain on the defensive. Something has already been said of the first case; and in the future we shall add whatever may seem necessary. Of the second case, nothing can be said except to encourage such princes to fortify and strengthen their walled cities, and to waste no thought on the surrounding countryside. Whoever shall have fortified his walled town well, and who has conducted his other affairs with his subjects in the manner indicated above—and as will be indicated further as we proceed —will always be attacked only with the greatest circumspection. For men are always opposed to undertakings in which they foresee difficulties, and certainly none can consider it an easy matter to assault one who has his walled city strongly fortified and is not hated by his people.

The cities of Germany enjoy the greatest freedom,[18] have little dependent countryside about them, and obey the emperor only when they want to. They stand in fear neither of him nor of any other of the powerful lords who surround them, because they are so strongly fortified that everyone realizes that an assault upon them must prove a long, drawn-out and difficult affair. They all have suitable walls and moats and adequate artillery; they always keep food, drink and fuel to last a year in readiness in public storehouses. In addition, to keep the people fed without drain on the public funds, they hold in reserve a year's supply of those materials which make it possible for the people to work at those trades which are the nerve and life of that particular city, and at the occupations by which the common people earn their sustenance. Furthermore, they place a high value upon military exercises and make many provisions for them.

A prince therefore who has a strong city and who does not make himself hated, cannot be attacked;

and if perchance someone does attack him, he will
soon withdraw from the undertaking with shame.
The events of the world are so variable that it is
impossible that anyone would be able to engage his
forces in laying siege to his city for a year. Someone
may object that if the people have their possessions
outside the walls and watch them put to the flame,
they surely will lose patience and the long seige and
their own self-interest will make them forget their
prince. I reply that a powerful and resourceful prince
will overcome all those difficulties now fanning the
hope of his subjects that the evil will not endure for
long, now arousing in them fear at the thought of the
ferocity of the enemy; and again by taking precautions against those who seem to him to be too impetuous. In addition, the enemy, reasonably enough,
will have to set fire to and lay waste the countryside
when he first opens the siege, and this at a time when
the spirits of the defenders are still inflamed and
eager. The prince therefore has even less reason to
worry about this point, because by the time that their
spirits have grown cold after a few days of siege, the
damage has already been done, the evils have been
sustained, and there is no longer any remedy for it.
The people thereupon draw in to a closer unity with
their ruler, for now that their houses have been
burned and their possessions destroyed in his defense,
they will feel that he has a greater obligation toward
them. And the nature of men is such that they feel as
much obligated by the good they do as by the benefits
they receive. Therefore, if everything is weighed carefully, it should not be difficult for a prudent prince
to keep the spirits of his citizens firm both at the
beginning of a siege and as its course continues, when
neither the means of life nor those of defense are
lacking.

XI

Ecclesiastical Principalities

There only remains for us now to discuss ecclesiastical principalities. All the difficulties which these present occur before possession of them is secured. They are acquired by fortune or by personal capacity, but are maintained without the one or the other. For they are sustained by the ancient institutions of religion which are so powerful and of such character that they maintain their princes in power no matter how they conduct themselves or what kind of life they live. They alone have states but do not defend them, and subjects whom they do not govern. And their states, because they are undefended, are not taken from them, while their subjects, because they are not governed, take no heed of these matters and neither can nor do conspire to be separated from them. Consequently only these principalities are happy and secure. But since they are ruled by a higher principle, which the human mind cannot fathom, I shall not speak about them. Raised up and maintained by God, it would be presumptuous and rash to discourse upon them. Nevertheless, if anyone should ask how the Church in the temporal order has come to such a position of power, despite the fact that up to the time of [Pope] Alexander the Italian potentates—and not only those who were really powerful, but every insignificant baron and lord—thought her temporal power of little importance, I shall not deem it superfluous to record in substance, how this has come about even though it may be well known. Even today a king of France trembles before it, because she has been able drive him out of Italy and bring the Venetians to ruin.

Before Charles, King of France, invaded Italy, that country was under the domination of the pope, the Venetians, the King of Naples, the Duke of Milan and the Florentines. These powers were preoccupied with two principal concerns: the first, lest a foreigner should enter Italy in force, the second lest one or another among themselves should extend his domain. Those who were most concerned on these points were the pope and the Venetians, while to keep the Venetians in check the union of all the others was necessary, as the example of Ferrara proved.[19] It was the function of the barons of Rome to keep the power of the pope within limits. As these barons were divided into two factions, the Orsini and the Colonna, there was always occasion for strife between them. While thus armed under the very eyes of the pope, they inevitably kept him weak and powerless. And even though, from time to time, a spirited pope would appear, such as Sixtus, still none of these ever enjoyed either the good fortune or the personal capacity to deliver himself from that difficult situation. The briefness of the average reign of a pope also contributed to this situation. In the ten years, on the average, during which a pope might reign, he might, with considerable expenditure of effort, reduce the position of one of those factions. For example, if one pope had practically destroyed the power of the Colonnas, he would be succeeded by another hostile to the Orsini who would proceed to restore the power of the Colonnas, without at the same time being able to put down the Orsini. The result of all this was that the temporal powers of the pope were held of little importance in Italy. Then, however, Alexander VI ascended the papal throne. Of all the popes who have ever reigned, he showed how much a pope, with money and armed forces, could prevail. And he achieved, through the agency of the Duke of Valentino and the opportunity offered by the withdrawal of the French, all those things of which I have spoken above in describing the undertakings of the Duke. And even though his purpose was not to exalt the Church but the Duke, nevertheless, what he actually achieved redounded to the greatness of the Church which, after his death and the ruin of the Duke, remained the beneficiary of their labors.

There succeeded him Pope Julius, who found the Church already great, in possession of the whole of the Romagna, the barons of Rome crushed and the factions among them reduced to impotence by [Pope] Alexander's efforts. He also found means already prepared of accumulating money which had never been used by any pope before Alexander. And Julius not only took advantage of these opportunities but improved them. He planned to gain possession of Bologna, to crush the Venetians and to drive the French out of Italy. And all these undertakings proved successful and all the more to his praise, because he did everything to exalt the Church and nothing for his own private gain. He kept the Orsini and the Colonna factions within the limits to which he had found them reduced. Although there were among them some who would have liked to change things, two considerations kept them in check: the first, the very greatness of the Church which tended to overawe them; and second, the fact that the College of Cardinals had no members from among them. The Cardinals are the causes of disturbances among them, for they foster factional disputes within and outside Rome so that the barons are forced to come to their defense. Thus the ambitions of prelates stir up discord and tumults among the barons. His Holiness Pope Leo found the pontificate very powerful. It is to be hoped that as his predecessors made it powerful by the force of their arms, he may, by his goodness and numberless other virtues, raise it to the heights of grandeur and veneration.

XII

The Number of Types of Military Organization and Mercenary Troops

I have discussed in particular all of the characteristics of those principalities about which in the beginning I proposed to talk, considered in some degree the reasons why they prosper and decline, and demonstrated the ways in which many persons have sought to obtain and to retain them. It remains for me now to discuss in a general way the means of offense and defense which may be employed in each of them. We have pointed out above how necessary it is for a prince to lay the foundations of his power solidly and how, lacking these, he must inevitably come to ruin. And the principle foundations which all states have—whether new or old or composite—are good laws and powerful armies. And since there can be no good laws where there are not strong armies, while where the armies are strong the laws will necessarily be good, I shall set aside any discussion of laws and proceed to speak of armies.

I say therefore that the armed forces with which a prince defends his position of power are either his own or mercenary troops, auxilary or composite. Mercenary soldiers and auxiliaries are dangerous and useless; and if a prince bases his state on mercenary troops, he will never be firm nor secure in his position.

For these troops are disunited, ambitious, without discipline, unfaithful. Strong among their friends, among enemies treacherous, they know neither fear of God nor fidelity toward men. The ruin they inevitably bring is deferred only so long as battle is put off; in peace one is despoiled by them as in war he is despoiled by an enemy. The reason for this is clear. They have no other attachment nor any other reason to keep them in the field than a meager pay, which is not enough to insure any desire to die for you. They are willing enough to be your soldiers so long as you wage no war. When war comes, they either flee or desert. It should take little to persuade any observing person of the truth of what I say; for the havoc which prevails in Italy today is due to no other cause than the fact that for many years it has relied on mercenary troops. These troops did make some progress for one prince or another and seemed strong enough when fighting each other.[20] However, when foreign troops entered they quickly showed what they really were. As a result it was possible for Charles, King of France, to take Italy with a piece of chalk, that is, simply by billeting his men about. And the man who had the courage to tell us that the reasons for this were our own sins and faults was telling the truth.* These faults were not the ones which he alleged, however, but the failings which I have just narrated. And since they were the sins of princes, the princes have suffered for them.[21]

I would like to point out even more clearly the evils involved in the use of these troops. The mercenary captains are either capable men, or they are not. When they are, you can put no faith in them, for they will always be looking to their own aggrandizement, either by crushing you, their master, or by crushing

* Machiavelli is here referring to Savonarola.

others beyond those it was your intention that they should defeat. If such a captain is not capable, he will ruin you almost as a matter of course. And if some one should protest that any men of arms, whether mercenary or not, will do the same, I will reply that armed forces must be under the control either of a prince or of a republic. A prince must take personal command of his forces; the republic must appoint commanders from among its own citizens. And when one of these does not prove to be effective, it must replace him at once. When he does prove effective, provision should be made by law that he must not go beyond the task, or exercise greater power, than initially assigned him. Experience shows that only armed princes and armed republics make notable advances and that mercenary troops bring nothing but woes. A republic guarded by its own citizen army is far less apt to be subjugated by one of its own citizens than a republic armed with forces not its own.

Rome and Sparta endured for many centuries, armed and free. The Swiss are heavily armed and completely free. The Carthaginians offer an example of the poor results of the use of mercenary troops in ancient times. They were almost subjugated by their mercenary troops after the first war with the Romans, even though the Carthaginians had their own citizens as captains. After the death of Epaminondas, Phillip of Macedon was placed in command of their forces by the Thebans. After winning their victory, he stripped them of their liberty. The citizens of Milan, after the death of Duke Philip, engaged Francesco Sforza to fight against the Venetians. After defeating the enemy at Caravaggio, he allied himself with them in order to subjugate his original employers, the Milanese. The father of this same Sforza, after entering the service of Queen Giovanna of Naples, deserted her without warning, leaving her unarmed and defenseless. As a result, to save her kingdom, she had to throw herself on the mercy of the King of Aragon.

If it is pointed out that before these events the Venetians and the Florentines had both enlarged their dominions through the employment of mercenary troops, whose captains defended them and did not try to make themselves masters, I reply that the Florentines were in this instance favored by chance. Of the competent commanders they engaged and of whom they had reason to be afraid, some were not victorious, some met opposition, others turned their ambitions elsewhere. The one who was not victorious was Giovanni Acuto; and in the circumstances, his loyalty could not be put to a test. But everyone recognizes that had he been successful the Florentines would have been at his mercy. The Sforzas were always in competition with the Bracceschi and so they served as a check upon each other. Francesco Sforzo turned his ambitions upon Lombardy, Braccio against the Church and the realm of Naples. But let us consider what happened only a short time ago. The Florentines made Paolo Vitelli their commander. He was a very prudent man who had risen to high reputation from the status of a private citizen. Had this man sacked Pisa, there is no one who would deny that the Florentines would have had to go along with his plans. For had he then gone over to the service of their enemies they would have had no defense against him, while if they had retained his services, they would have ended up obeying him. If one considers the progress made by the Venetians he will see that they operated securely and with glory to themselves only so long as they waged war with their own troops;

the combination of the patricians and the armed plebians proved most effective. This, however, was before they turned to enterprises on the mainland. When they undertook this step, they lost their advantage and followed the pattern already established in Italy. At the opening of these undertakings on the mainland, they did not have a great deal to fear from their captains, since they had small possessions to risk there and still enjoyed a great reputation. As they extended their acquisitions on the mainland, as they did under Carmagnola, they had a taste of this mistake. They had evidence of his capacity, for under his leadership they had defeated the Duke of Milan. They had also acquired information from other sources that he had become less interested in the war. As a consequence, they concluded that they could win no more battles under his leadership. However, since they did not wish—or better could not afford—to free him from their services, lest they lose what they had acquired, they had to kill him. Thereafter they retained as commanders Bartolommeo da Bergamo, Ruberto di San Severino, Count of Pitigliano, and other men of this calibre. Under their leadership, the Venetians had to be more concerned lest they lose what they had acquired than with the hope of further gains. And the event at Vailà bore out their concern, for there, in a single engagement, they lost what it had taken eight centuries and immense cost to acquire. Gains through the use of mercenary troops are slow, belated and uncertain, while the defeats to which they lead are sudden and defy explanation. Since I have been led by these examples to speak of Italy which for many years has been dominated by mercenary troops, I would like to discuss these matters in more general terms so that when the origin and progress of these errors is seen, better provision may be made against them.

You must then understand that as soon as the empire began to lose its hold on Italy in these latter times, and that the papacy began to gain greater stature in temporal affairs, Italy became divided into many states. Many of the larger cities took up arms, with the favor of the emperor, against the nobles, who formerly had oppressed them. To increase its own prestige, the Church supported the towns. In many other towns, one or another of the citizens became prince. Hence it was that, since Italy had fallen into the hands of the Church and these republics and since the priests and the citizens of the cities had no experience in warfare, they began to hire foreigners as mercenary troops. The first man who brought reputation to this kind of military force was Alberigo da Conio from the Romagna. Among others, Braccio and Sforza, who in their days were the arbiters of Italy, followed his example. In their wake came all the others who, down to our own day, have led such troops. The result of their power has been that Italy has been invaded from one end to the other by Charles, plundered by Louis, assaulted by Ferrando and put to shame by the Swiss. The policy which has guided them has been to gain prestige for themselves, at the expense of that of the infantry. They did this because, as men without countries, working for hire, a few foot soldiers could gain them no standing and they could not provide support for large numbers of them. They therefore concentrated on cavalry, for with a supportable number of horsemen they gained both riches and reputation. Things came to such a pass that in an army of twenty thousand soldiers less than two thousand foot soldiers were to be found. They had, moreover, used every device to ease their own task and danger, as well as those of their followers. Instead of slaying the enemy in battles, they took prisoners without demanding ransom. They would not attack fortified towns by night; those who defended such towns would not make sorties from them. They did not build barricades or dig moats around their camps; they would not take the field in winter. And all these things were stipulated in their military codes and were thought up by them in order, as I have said, to reduce danger and hardship to such an extent that they have brought Italy to her present condition of enslavement and dishonor.

XIII

Auxiliary, Composite, and Native Troops

Auxiliary troops, the second of the kinds which we have called useless, are those obtained by appealing to some strong prince for aid. Pope Julius took this course in very recent times. He turned to auxiliary troops when, in his undertaking against Ferrara, he had sad experience of the temper of his mercenaries and Ferdinand, King of Spain, had to come to his aid with men and troops.[22] Such troops may be useful and effective in themselves, but they are almost always disastrous for one who appeals to them. If they are defeated, he is undone; if victorious, he finds himself in their power. Although the ancient histories provide many examples of this, I prefer to dwell on this recent example of Pope Julius, whose

decision—imposed by his desire to capture Ferrara—
to place himself in the hands of a foreigner could not
have been more poorly conceived. His good fortune,
however, favored him with a third circumstance; as
the result of which he did not have to reap the fruit of
his ill-considered decision. The auxiliary troops he
sent were indeed destroyed at Ravenna; but the Swiss
intervened and drove off the victors. Contrary to his
own expectations and those of everyone else, [Pope]
Julius did not fall prisoner to the enemy, who had
fled before the Swiss, nor to his own auxiliaries, since
he had emerged victorious through other arms than
theirs. The Florentines, who were entirely without
native forces, hired ten thousand French soldiers to
destroy Pisa. Through this decision they incurred
greater dangers than any others they knew through
all their troubled times. The emperor of Constantinople, to protect himself against his neighbors, sent
ten thousand Turks against Greece. After the campaign, these refused to leave and in this way Greece
fell into slavery to the infidels.[23]

Anyone, consequently, who does not want military
victory, should turn to troops of this kind, for they
are much more dangerous even than mercenaries.
The source of the ruin they bring lies in this: they
constitute a united force, but wholly obedient to
others than yourself. Mercenaries, even after they
have been victorious, need more time and greater
opportunity to do injury to you, because they do not
constitute a united body and because they have been
assembled by you and are in your pay. Under these
circumstances, the third person, whom you may have
placed at their head, cannot in a short time achieve
such authority among them that he can turn it against
you. To sum up, it is cowardice which makes merce-

nary troops dangerous, but their very strength con-
stitutes a peril in auxiliaries.

A wise prince, consequently, has always avoided
recourse to this kind of troops, relying rather on his
own men. And he has preferred to lose with his own,
rather than win with the troops of others, realizing
that that can be no true victory which is secured with
alien forces. I shall never hesitate to cite Cesare
Borgia and his manner of proceeding as an example.
The Duke entered the Romagna with auxiliary troops
of French origin, and with them took Imola and Forlí.
Realizing that these troops were not trustworthy, he
turned to mercenaries, considering them to be less
dangerous, and hired the Orsini and Vitelli. As he
employed these, he learned that they too were untrust-
worthy, unfaithful and dangerous, so he dispensed
with their services and turned to his own forces. And
the difference between these types of troops can
be the better appreciated, if one considers the altera-
tion in the Duke's reputation when he had only the
French, when he had the Orsini and the Vitelli, and
when finally he relied only on his own forces and on
himself. His reputation underwent a constant im-
provement as these changes took place. And he
finally reached his full stature, when everyone saw
that he was sole master of his own armed forces.

I did not intend to depart from Italian examples
drawn from recent experience; nevertheless, I find it
impossible completely to pass over that of Hiero of
Syracuse, whom I mentioned earlier. This man, as
I have recounted, was placed in command of the
armed forces of the Syracusans. He realized at once
that those mercenary troops were of no use at all;
for they were hired troops organized much like our
Italian companies. Understanding that he could neither control nor disband them, he had them all cut to

pieces. Thereafter, he made war with his own troops and never with alien forces. I would also like to recall to memory a figure of the Old Testament, one almost made to illustrate this argument. When David presented himself to Saul offering to do battle with the Philistine champion, Saul, to give him courage, offered him the use of his own armour. But David, after trying it on, refused the offer, protesting that with it he could not make use of his own prowess effectively. He preferred to seek out the enemy with only his own sling and knife.

In fine, the arms of another either fall from your back or so weigh you down that your movements are impeded. After Charles VIII, the father of King Louis XI, had through good fortune and personal enterprise liberated France from the English, he appreciated this necessity of commanding his own armed forces and so was led to initiate the organization of cavalry and infantry units. Later, King Louis expanded the infantry and began to hire Swiss troops. This mistake and others which followed, proved, as we can see today, the cause of grave reverses to his kingdom. By according such importance to the Swiss, he lessened the reputation of his own forces; the native infantry has been disbanded completely and the mounted troops made dependent on foreign troops. As the mounted troops became accustomed to fighting with Swiss help, they came gradually to believe that they could not win without it. As a result, the French cannot prevail against the Swiss and without the Swiss are no match for anyone else. The armies of France, therefore, have been composite, that is, partly mercenary and partly native. Such armies, taken as a whole, are superior to those which are all mercenary or all auxiliary, but still much inferior to those composed entirely of one's own forces. The example cited should suffice to establish this truth. The Kingdom of France would have proven unconquerable had the military institutions of Charles been retained and improved. But the imprudence of men leads them to take up something, because at the moment it tastes good, and they do not detect the poison which it conceals within; just as I noted above about severe fevers.

The prince, therefore, who does not recognize evils at their very birth, is not truly a wise prince; yet this discernment is given to few. And if one considers the first stage of the weakening of the Roman empire, it will be found to have begun with the hiring of the Goths as mercenary troops.[24] With this expedient, the native forces of the Roman empire began to be devitalized; and all the prowess which departed the Romans, passed over to the Goths. I conclude, therefore, that unless it possesses its own armed forces, no principality is secure. On the contrary, it is wholly at the mercy of fortune, without internal resources in times of adversity. And it has always been the opinion and maxim of wise men: "quod nihil sit tam infirmum aut instabile quam fama potentiae non sua vi nixa: that nothing is so weak or unstable as a reputation for power which does not rest on one's own forces." [25] By one's own forces we mean those which are composed either of subjects, or citizens or one's own dependents. All other types are either mercenaries or auxiliaries. It is easy to discover the proper manner of organizing one's own forces if one studies the procedures of the four men whom I have named above and considers how Phillip, the father of Alexander the Great, and many republics and princes have armed and organized themselves. I defer completely to the wisdom of those institutions.

XIV

What a Prince Should Do About His Military Forces

A prince, therefore, should have no other object, nor any other thought, nor take as his own special art any other concern than war, its institutions and discipline; for that is the only art which belongs properly to one who holds ruling power. And that is so efficacious that it not only maintains in their positions those who are rulers by right of birth, but often makes it possible for men of private station to rise to positions of power. Contrariwise, it is readily seen that when princes have paid more attention to the refinements of life than to war, they have lost their positions of power. The prime cause which makes you lose power is neglect of this art; and the prime factor which makes it possible for you to acquire power, is mastery of this art.

Francesco Sforza, by reason of his armed might, rose from private station to become Duke of Milan, while his sons, because they neglected the exercises of war, fell rapidly from the position of dukes to that of private persons. Among the other reasons why inexpertness in war must beget evil for you is that it leads people to hold you in contempt. This is one of those infamies against which a prince must be on his guard, as I will stress presently. For between one versed in war and one inexpert in that art, there is no comparison; nor is it according to sound common sense for an armed man freely to obey one who is unarmed, or that one unversed in arms should feel secure among servitors who know that art. The one will be touched with disdain, the other suspicious; as a consequence, it is not possible for them to cooperate effectively. Finally, a prince who does not understand the art of war, in addition to his other misfortunes which we have noted, will never be esteemed by his soldiers nor ever be able to put his entire trust in them.

The prince should never permit his mind to be distracted from the thought of the art of war, and in times of peace he ought to study it with even greater care than in times of actual hostilities. He can do this in two ways: the first by his actions, the second by his thoughts. So far as his actions are concerned, in addition to maintaining his armed forces well organized and exercised, he ought constantly to engage in the hunt so as to accustom his body to all kinds of hardship. He should also learn to study the nature of terrain, come to know how the mountains rise, how the valleys open out, how the plains lie, and understand the nature of rivers and marshes. Such studies should engage his most serious attention, for such knowledge is useful in two ways: first, by it he comes to know the character of his own territory and thus how better to defend it; secondly, through knowledge of and exercise in his own territory, he can come readily to understand any other area which it might become necessary for him to reconnoitre. For the hills, valleys and plains, rivers and marshes of Tuscany, for example, bear a certain likeness to those of other areas. As a consequence, from the knowledge of the terrain of one's own province, one readily infers the character of another. The prince who lacks this kind of experience, lacks the first requirement of a leader. For thus he learns how to find out the enemy, select his own campsites, conduct his armies on the march, select points of encounter, arrange advantageous battle order, and lay siege to fortified places, all to his own advantage.

Philopoemen, prince of the Achaeans, among the other praises heaped upon him by the historians, is renowned especially for this: that in time of peace he thought only of the art of waging war. When he was walking in the fields with his friends, he would frequently stop to discuss these matters with them, setting them such problems as these: if the enemy had taken up his position on that hill, and we found ourselves here in this spot with our armies, which of us would have the advantage? how would we go about, while holding our ranks, scouting his position? if we decided to withdraw, what measures would we take? if they were to withdraw, how would we organize the pursuit? And as he walked along with them he would lay before them all the various situations in which an army might find itself. He would listen to their opinions and state his own, supporting them with arguments drawn from his great experience. The result of this ceaseless preoccupation was that never in leading his army did there ever arise a situation for which he did not have a ready solution.

As to the exercise of the mind, the prince should peruse histories and, in doing so, meditate upon the actions of great men, noting how they conducted themselves in war; examine the reason for their victories and their defeats as well, in order to avoid the latter and to imitate the former. Above all he should do what other excellent men have done in the past: select some one historical figure, who has been honored and praised, as his special model, keeping his work always before his mind's eye. It is said that Alexander the Great thus imitated Achilles, Caesar, Alexander, Scipio, and Cyrus. And anyone who has read the life of Cyrus written by Xenophon will recognize in the life of Scipio how much glory that imitation brought him, and how much in his restraint, affability, humanity and liberality Scipio reflected what Xenophon had written about Cyrus. The wise prince should act in the same way; he should never be idle in time of peace but by his activity should, as it were, make capital of times of peace so that he might draw upon it in times of adversity. And [thus] whatever countenance fortune should present, she will find him ready to meet her.

XV

The Things for Which Men and Especially Princes Are Praised and Blamed

It remains now to consider the manner in which a prince should conduct himself toward his subjects and his friends. I know that many writers have treated this topic, so that I am somewhat hesitant in taking it up in my turn lest I appear presumptuous, especially because in what I shall have to say, I shall depart from rules which other writers have laid down. Since it is my intention to write something which may be of real utility to anyone who can comprehend it, it has appeared to me more urgent to penetrate to the effective reality of these matters than to rest content with mere constructions of the imagination. For many writers[26] have constructed imaginary republics and principalities which have never been seen nor known actually to exist. But so wide is the separation between the way men actually live and the way that they ought to live, that anyone who turns his attention from what is actually done to what ought to be done, studies his own ruin rather than his preservation. Any man who wishes to make a profession of goodness in every department of conduct, must inevitably come to ruin among so many men who are not good. Therefore a ruler who wishes to preserve his power must learn to be able not to be good, and to use this knowledge or not use it as necessity may dictate.

Setting aside therefore all vain imaginings about what a prince ought to be and centering our discussion on things as they really are, I submit that all men, and especially princes by their high position, when discussion of their merit arises, are measured according to certain qualities the possession or reputation for which earns them either praise or censure. Thus it is that one is thought liberal, another miserly —using this word in the Tuscan sense, because "avaro" in our language still indicates one who wants to acquire possessions by plunder, while we call one "misero" who abstains too much from the use of what he possesses—another is held to be a benefactor, another a plunderer; one cruel, another compassionate; one faithless to his word, another faithful; one effeminate and lacking in spirit, another full of spirit to the point of rashness; one man is considered courteous, another haughty; one lascivious, another chaste; one, of single intention, another crafty and conniving; one obstinate, another amenable; one grave, another light-hearted; one religious, another unbelieving and so forth. Everyone would of course hold that it would be a most laudable thing in a prince to be possessed of all the favorable qualities enumerated above, but all of these cannot be possessed at once, nor observed in their entirely, for the conditions of human life do not permit this. A prince must therefore be prudent enough to know how to avoid any derogatory reputation for those qualities which might lead him to lose his power, and to be on his guard against those qualities which do carry this danger, in so far as he finds it possible. And if he cannot avoid them, he can tolerate them in himself without too much concern for consequences. Even more, however, he must not draw back from incurring a reputation for those vices without which his position cannot be maintained without difficulty; the reason is that, when the entire matter is considered carefully, certain qualities which appear to be virtues, when practiced will lead to his ruin; while the pursuit of others, which seem to be vices, will insure his own security and the stability of his position.

XVI

Liberality and Parsimony

I shall begin then with the first of the above mentioned qualities, agreeing that it would indeed be most advantageous to be considered liberal; nevertheless, liberality, if exercised in such a way that you come to be held a free-spending man, may do you harm. This quality, if exercised as a virtue—as it ought to be—will not be obvious, and hence will not prevent your being accused of its contrary. If one wishes to keep up a name for liberality among men, one must not omit any kind of lavish display; however, if he indulges in such display, it will consume all his resources. In the end, he will be forced to place exorbitant burdens upon his people, to resort to excessive taxes and have recourse to such other expedients as may increase revenue in order to maintain this reputation. This mode of conduct will soon begin to earn him the hatred of his subjects, and general contempt when he reaches the point of impoverishment. In addition, his liberality will have benefited few, while offending many. As a consequence, he will be vulnerable at many points and the first real peril will prove a disaster. And, to fill up the measure of this irony, if the prince, realising these dangers, tries to withdraw from such a position, he will immediately be marked down as a miser.

Since a prince cannot exercise this virtue of liberality without danger to himself, except by ostentation, he ought not to be concerned about being thought a miser. With the passage of time, he will gradually acquire a reputation for liberality, when it is seen that by cautious expenditure his revenues always are sufficient to his needs, that he is always prepared to repel anyone who attacks him, and that he can carry through his undertakings without imposing exorbitant burdens on his people. All those from whom he takes nothing will deem him liberal, and they will be numerous; all those to whom he gives nothing will think him miserly, but they will be few. In our own days, we have seen that only those who have been thought misers have achieved great things; the others have all exhausted themselves in vain. Pope Julius, though he took advantage of a reputation for liberality to gain the papacy, on attaining it made no pretense of keeping up that reputation, because he was concerned with being able to carry on his wars.[27] The present king of France[28] wages almost constant warfare without imposing any extraordinary taxes on his country, because his long practice of parsimony had hoarded the means of meeting these added expenditures. The present King of Spain,[29] had he cultivated liberality, would never have been able to achieve as much or carry out successfully so many great undertakings as he had done.

Consequently a prince ought to deem a reputation for miserliness a small thing if it frees him from the necessity of oppressing his subjects, enables him to defend himself, and prevents his becoming poor, despised and rapacious. It is one of those qualities which makes it possible to maintain power. And should someone protest that Caesar rose to imperial power through his reputation for liberality, and many others who enjoyed the reputation for being liberal—and have in fact been so—have risen to the highest positions, I must reply as follows: either you are already a prince or you are in the process of acquiring political power. In the first instance, liberality is a source of danger; in the second instance, however, it is indeed necessary to have a reputation for being liberal. Caesar was one of the competitors for the supreme power in Rome; if, having achieved that power, he had survived but not tempered his vast expenditures, he would have destroyed his position. And if someone else insists: many have been the princes who have had great military success and yet enjoyed the reputation for liberality, I must answer you: the prince expends either his own and his subjects' resources, or those of others. In the first case he is well advised to be frugal; in the second case, he should pass up no opportunity of displaying liberality. The prince who takes the field with his armies and maintains them by raids, by sacking cities and by extortions, is disposing of the resources of others and must display liberality or his soldiers may refuse to follow him. Of that which is not your own or your subjects' you may well be the free dispenser, as were Cyrus, Caesar and Alexander; for it does no harm to your reputation but even adds to it. The only thing which brings you harm is to squander your own resources. There is nothing which consumes itself so completely as liberality; even as you exercise it, you lose the power to exercise it. As a result you become either poor and despised or—to escape these consequences—rapacious and hence hated. Contempt and hatred are the two things which above all others a prince must avoid; and liberality will earn you both. Therefore it is wiser to be thought a miser, which brings infamy but not hatred, than, through the desire to be known as a liberal man, to be forced to incur a reputation for rapaciousness, which brings ignominy *and* hatred.

XVII

Cruelty and Compassion and Whether It Is Better to Be Loved than Feared or the Opposite

Coming down now to the other qualities mentioned above, I submit that every prince ought to want to be considered compassionate rather than cruel. At the same time, he must avoid an ill-advised use of compassion. Cesare Borgia was thought cruel; nevertheless, that cruelty of his had restored the Romagna, united it, brought it peace and reduced it to obedience. If one considers the matter carefully, it will be seen that he was in fact much more compassionate than were the Florentines who, in order to avoid being thought cruel, permitted Pistoia to be destroyed. Therefore, a prince ought not to permit a reputation for cruelty to disturb him, if it is the price of keeping his subjects united and obedient. By making examples of a few, he will prove in the end more compassionate than those who, through excess of compassion, permit disorders to arise, which prove in turn the source of murders and violence. For the latter outrages inevitably arouse the entire community, while those few executions which the prince may impose harm only certain persons in particular. Among all princes, it is most nearly impossible for the new prince to avoid a reputation for cruelty, simply because new states are exposed to so many dangers. As Virgil [30] says through the lips of Dido:

> Res dura et regni novitas me talia cogunt
> Moliri et late fines custode tueri.

> Harsh necessity and the newness of my kingdom force me to do such things and to guard my frontiers on every side (Aeneid I 563-4).

Nevertheless, he should be considerate in lending credence and in committing himself to action, nor should he become fearful of his own shadow. He should proceed in a temperate manner, with prudence and humanity, so that over confidence will not make him rash nor will excessive distrustfulness render him unbearable.

From this circumstance, an argument arises: whether it is better to be loved rather than feared, or the opposite. The answer is that one would like to be both one and the other; but since they are difficult to combine, it is more secure to be feared than loved, when one of the two must be surrendered. For it may be said of men in general, that they are ingrates, fickle, deceivers, evaders of danger, desirous of gain. So long as you are doing good for any of them they are all yours, offering you their blood, goods, lives, children, when any real necessity for doing so is remote, but turning away when such need draws near, as I have remarked. The prince who relies wholly on their words, and takes no other precautions, will come to ruin. Friendships gained at a price and not founded on greatness and nobility of soul, are indeed purchased but never possessed; and in times of need cannot be drawn upon. Men are less concerned about giving offense to one who goes about making himself loved than to one who makes himself feared; love is a bond of obligation which men—sad creatures that they are—break on the first occasion touching their own interests; but fear binds by a threat of punishment which never relaxes. Still, the prince should take care to make himself feared in due measure; though he merits not love, he should avoid being hated. (His position is strongest when he is feared but not hated.) And he will establish such a relationship if he does not despoil his subjects of their goods and keeps his hands off their women. Even when it is necessary for him to proceed against the blood-kin of anyone, he must make it clear that he does so only for manifest cause and with commensurate justification. Above all, let him keep his hands off others' property, because men forget the death of their own fathers more readily that the loss of their patrimonies. Moreover, pretexts for seizing another's property are never lacking; and one who begins to live by plunder, never fails to find a reason for seizing another's property. Justifications for taking a life, however, present themselves more rarely and are much less convincing.

When the prince is in the field with his armies, directing large numbers of men, it is quite necessary that a reputation for cruelty cause him no concern. Without such a reputation, he can never keep an army united or prevent if from falling into factions. Among Hannibal's most notable achievements must surely be accounted the fact that, though he commanded a very numerous army, drawn from a large diversity of races and led it to battle in foreign lands, no dissention ever arose within its ranks, either between portions of the army or against the commander, either in good or in adverse circumstances. The only thing able to account for this must have been his inhuman cruelty which, together with his inexhaustible resourcefulness, made him an object of terror and veneration to the eyes of his soldiers. The historians who have not analyzed this matter well have given a confused impression of it; on the one hand, admiring his mode of conduct and, on the other, condemning the only quality which could have assured it. To appreciate the fact that none of Hannibal's other qualities could have accounted for this achievement, one need only consider the case of Scipio, whose armies in Spain mutinied against him, a very rare occurrence, not only in his own times, but in the whole of recorded history. The only reason which can account for that mutiny was his excessive compassion, which had led him to grant his soldiers a greater freedom than is consonant with military life. This was the basis of his censure in the Senate by Fabius Maximus, who called him a corrupter of the Roman Army. When one of his legates destroyed Locri without his orders he neither revenged its destruction nor censured the legate, his excessive good nature preventing the one action and the other.[31] A colleague in the Senate recognized this failing when, in Scipio's defense, he pointed out that there are many men who know better how to avoid an error than how to correct one. This quality of his character would in time have destroyed Scipio's fame and glory, had he conducted himself in this way while exercising the supreme power, the *imperium*. But living as he did under the government of the Senate, this damaging characteristic was not only concealed, but counted as an element of his glory.

Returning to the question of being loved or feared, I conclude that since men give their affection as they please, but yield to fear because the prince inspires it, a wise prince will rest his power on that which is his to control, not on that which lies in the power of others. His only concern must be to avoid being hated, as has been said.

XVIII

How Princes Should Observe Good Faith

Everyone understands well enough how praiseworthy it is in a prince to keep his word, to live with integrity and not by guile. Nevertheless, the experience of our times teaches us that those princes have achieved great things who have looked upon the keeping of one's word as a matter of little moment and have understood how, by their guile, to twist men's minds; and in the end have surpassed those who have rested their power upon faithfulness.

You ought to understand therefore that there are two ways of fighting, the one by the laws, the other with force. The first is proper to men, the second to beasts; but since in many instances the first is not enough, it is necessary to have recourse to the second. A prince, consequently, must understand how to use the manner proper to the beast as well as that proper to man. This truth has been taught to princes by the writers of ancient times covertly. Thus they described how Achilles and many other of those princes of ancient times were sent to be brought up by the centaur Chiron and educated under his tutelage. To have as teacher a creature half man and half beast means nothing else than that a prince must know how to use the one nature and the other, and that without the one, the other cannot endure.

Since, then, a prince must of necessity know how to use the bestial nature, he should take as his models from among beasts the fox and the lion; for the lion does not defend himself from traps, and the fox does not defend himself from the wolves. One must therefore be a fox to scent out the traps and a lion to ward off the wolves. Those who act simply the lion do not understand the implications of their own actions.[32] A prudent prince cannot—nor ought he—observe faith when such observance may turn against himself, and when the reasons which led him to pledge it have lost their force. If all men were good, this precept would not be valid; but since they are sorry creatures and would not keep faith with you, no obligation binds you to observe it toward them.

Moreover, a prince never lacks legitimate reasons which may impart a convincing color to his non-observance. One might adduce innumerable modern examples of this truth and show how many treaties of peace, how many promises, have been broken and rendered meaningless through the infidelity of princes. And the one who has known how to act the fox has always come off the better. It is also necessary to know how to lend this volpine nature an attractive color and to be a great simulator and dissimulator. Men are so simple and so responsive to present necessities that he who would deceive will always find another who will permit himself to be deceived.

There is one recent example which I cannot pass over in silence. [Pope] Alexander VI never acted otherwise, never thought of anything else than to deceive men; and he always found someone on whom he could practice this art. Never was there a man more convincing in his serious statements or in affirming some matter with more impressive oaths, or in observing them less. Nevertheless, his lies always succeeded, just as he intended them to, because he understood so well this dimension of worldly life.

A prince does not have to possess all of the above named qualities; but he must give the appearance of having them. Even more, I will venture to say that to possess them and to observe them constantly is to create a danger to oneself, but to *seem* to have them is always useful. Thus it is always useful to appear to be compassionate, faithful to one's word, humane, sincere, religious; and the prince should actually cultivate these qualities. But he must keep his mind so disposed that when it is necessary not to exercise them, you may be able and may know how to act in the opposite manner. And this must be understood, that a prince—and especially a new prince—cannot cultivate all those qualities which cause men to be considered good; for he must frequently, in order to maintain his position, act against good faith, against charity, humanity and religion. And still he must have a soul disposed to accommodate itself, as the winds and variations of fortune command. He must, as I have said, not desert the good, if he can abide by it, but must know how to enter upon the ways of evil if he must.

A prince must take care, therefore, that nothing ever issues from his lips which does not appear inspired by the five above mentioned qualities. He must appear, to those who see and hear him, all compassion, all fidelity, all sincerity and integrity, all religion. And nothing is more important than to give an *men do not*

under-

stand

appearance of possessing this last quality. Men, on the whole, judge more by the eye than by the hand; because anyone can see, but it is permitted to few to touch. Everyone sees what you seem to be, few understand what you really are; and those few are not eager to oppose themselves to the opinion of the masses, who have the majesty of the state to defend them. In the actions of all men, and especially of princes, where there is no judge to whom one can appeal, one must look to the result. Let the prince therefore concentrate on winning and maintaining the state. The means he employs will always be judged honorable and be praised by all; for the herd is always taken in by appearances and by results. And in the world, it is only the many who need be considered. The few find a place in the world, only when the many discover reasons for following them; and these reasons will always be the results of events. A certain prince of our own day, whom it is better not to name, never preaches anything but peace and good faith, while being the worst enemy of the one and of the other; and both the one and the other— had he ever observed them—would more than once have stripped him of reputation and power.

XIX

The Manner of Avoiding Hatred and Contempt

Since I have discussed the most important of the qualities mentioned above, I would like now to discuss the remaining ones briefly, under the general heading: that the prince must give thought to avoid-

ing those things which might make him an object of
hatred and contempt. If he does this, he will have
fulfilled the part of a prince and will find no danger
at all in any attribution to him of other vices. He will
be hated above all, as I have said, if he is rapacious
and usurps the goods of his subjects and seduces their
women. He should therefore abstain from such actions. The generality of men when deprived neither
of goods nor of honor, live contentedly; and one has
therefore to contend only with the ambitions of a few.
And these can be restrained easily in many different
ways. A number of characteristics will bring him into
contempt: fickleness, friviolity, effeminacy, coward-
liness, lack of resolution. Against these the prince
should be on his guard as he would against the plague.
His efforts should all be directed to lending to his
actions an appearance of greatness, high-spiritedness,
seriousness, strength. In the settlement of private
disputes among his subjects, he should see to it that
his decision is irrevocable; and he should promote
such an opinion of himself that no one would think
of deceiving or tricking him.

The prince who succeeds in creating such an impression of himself is held in high regard, and against
a man who is held in high repute it is difficult to stir
up a conspiracy or provoke an attack—so long, be
it understood, as he is an outstanding man and revered by his subjects. A prince should be fearful of
danger from two quarters: from within, on the part
of his subjects; from without, by reason of powerful
external forces. Against the latter, he can defend
himself with reliable armies and loyal allies. And internal affairs will always be more readily controlled
when external affairs are securely conducted, except
when a conspiracy has already caused internal dis-
turbance. Even when external relations are unset-

tled—if he has ordered matters and conducted his own life in the manner I have indicated—he will withstand all onslaughts, so long as he does not abandon his position, exactly as I have narrated of Nabid the Spartan. With relation to his subjects, his chief concern, in the absence of external disturbances, must be secret conspiracy within. The prince can secure himself sufficiently against this eventuality, if he avoids becoming hated or despised and if he keeps his people content under his rule. And the means to these ends have been discussed at length above. One of the most powerful safeguards against conspiracy available to the prince is to avoid being hated by the populace. The conspirator always believes that by the death of the prince he will satisfy the desires of the people. When he realizes, however, that such an action might arouse the people, he will not have the courage to go forward with such a design, for the difficulties confronting conspirators are numberless. Experience shows that there have been many attempted conspiracies, but that few have come to a happy issue. A conspirator cannot act alone, nor can he seek companions except among malcontents. As soon as you have laid bare your intentions to a malcontent, however, you have given him the means of finding satisfaction; for by revealing what you have confided, he can hope to secure all that he had wished for. Seeing what he has to gain from this point of view, and realizing also that the issue of your undertaking must of necessity be dubious and full of peril, that malcontent, to keep faith with you, would indeed have to be either a rare friend or a bitterly confirmed enemy of the prince.

To put the matter briefly, I submit that on the side of the conspirator there is fear, envy and expectation of ruinous punishment; on the side of the prince, however, there is the majesty of established power, the laws, the resources of friends and of the state to protect him. When to all these factors, there is added the benevolence of the people toward him, it is impossible that anyone should be so bold as to stir up a conspiracy. Whereas, ordinarily the conspirator is plagued by fears before the event, in this latter case he must also be fearful of what may come after the event. With the people against him—even should he succeed in his intent—he will have nowhere to turn for refuge.

It is possible to adduce an endless number of examples in this matter. I shall content myself, however, with only one which took place within the memory of our fathers. Annibale Bentivogli, the grandfather of the present Annibale, who ruled in Bologna, was murdered by the Canneschi in a conspiracy. The murdered man left no other heir than Giovanni, who was still in swaddling clothes. Immediately after the murder, the people rose up and annihilated the Canneschi. This was the fruit of the good will of the people which the Bentivogli had earned and enjoyed in those days. Even more, that goodwill was so great that, although no member of that family remained in Bologna able to take over the reins of government after the death of Annibale, it inspired even greater demonstrations. Word was received that there lived in Florence a descendent of the Bentivogli who, up to that moment, had been known as the son of a certain carpenter; the citizens of Bologna sought him out and conferred on him the ruling power in their city. He ruled there until Giovanni had reached the age when he could assume the government.

I conclude therefore that a prince should take little account of conspiracies when his people are well disposed toward him; when they are ill-disposed, however, and hate him, he has reason to fear everything and everyone. Well-organized states and wise princes have always sought by every means not to exasperate the nobles and to keep the people contented; this is one of the most important matters which must occupy a prince.

Among the well-organized and well-governed kingdoms of our own times is France. In that kingdom are to be found a large number of well-defined institutions on which the liberty and security of the king depend. Of these, the parliament with its authority must be counted the first.[33] The man who gave its constitution to that kingdom understood well the ambition and the insolence of the nobles and realized that they should have a bit in their mouth to control them. He also understood the great aversion which the people entertained toward the nobles, based on fear, and it was his intention to give them some security. At the same time, he did not wish to make this latter the especial concern of the king, lest it deprive him of his influence with the nobles—on the ground that he favored the people—or with the people—on the ground that he favored the great. Therefore, he established a third judge, who could without prejudice to the king hold down the nobles and favor the populace. This institution could not have been better devised or more prudently directed, nor could a greater basis for the security of the king and the kingdom been provided. From these observations another important conclusion can be drawn: that princes ought to delegate the administration of unpopular matters to others, while reserving to their own discretion those which involve the conferring of favors. Again I conclude that a prince ought to esteem the nobles, but not at the cost of making himself hated by the people.

It may seem to many persons that the lives and deaths of many of the Roman emperors provide examples contrary to my opinion; for some of them led consistently praiseworthy lives and exhibited outstanding traits of character and still fell from power; and even were done to death at the hands of their own people who conspired against them. In order to reply to these objections, I shall discuss the qualities of some of the emperors, making clear that the manner in which they fell from power was entirely in conformity with the analysis I have given above. I shall place under consideration matters which are well known to those who have studied the events of that period. I will be satisfied to limit my discussion to all of those emperors who succeeded to the imperial power from Marcus the Philosopher to Maximus[34]; these were Marcus Aurelius, Commodus, his son, Pertinax, Julian, Severus, Caracalla, his son, Macrinus, Heliogabalus, Alexander and Maximinus.

The first thing to be noted is that, whereas in other principalities it was necessary to contend only with the ambition of the nobles and the insolence of the people, the Roman emperors had to contend with a third factor, the cruelty and avarice of their soldiers. This was a most difficult thing to do and it brought about the downfall of many of them, for it was almost impossible to satisfy both soldiers and the people. The people loved peace and for this reason preferred unadventurous emperors; but the soldiers preferred a prince of military spirit, insolent, rapacious and cruel. They wanted such leaders to turn these qualities against the people so as to secure double pay and satisfy their own avarice and cruelty. The result was that those emperors who did not possess, either by nature or by cultivation, such authority and repute that they could hold in check both the one and the other of these elements, inevitably were ruined. The greater number of these emperors, and especially those who were in power for the first time—once they learned the difficulty of meeting such contrasting demands—preferred to satisfy the soldiers and counted little any injury done the people. This decision was inescapable for them. Since princes cannot escape being hated by some elements, they must first seek not to be hated by everyone. Failing this, they must bend every effort to avoid the enmity of the most powerful elements. Therefore those emperors who because they were new to power had need of extraordinary favors, allied themselves more readily with the soldiers than with the people. This proved to be advantageous or disadvantageous according to the ability of the particular emperor to maintain his own standing with his troops. These considerations explain why Marcus, Pertinax and Alexander—men of unadventurous temper, lovers of justice, enemies of cruelty, humane and benign—all met, from Marcus forward, a sad end. Only Marcus lived and died a highly honored man, and this was because he succeeded to the imperial power by hereditary right and did not have to acknowledge receiving it either from the soldiers or from the people. He also possessed many personal qualities which earned him something like veneration; as a result he was able to keep both elements within their proper bounds and was never hated or despised. But Pertinax was created emperor contrary to the will of the soldiers. And accustomed as they were to licentious living under Commodus, they were unable to tolerate the disciplined life which Pertinax sought to impose upon them; consequently, they conceived a fierce hatred for him to which was added contempt for his old age. And so, at the very outset of his administration, he lost power.

At this point we might pause to note that hatred *good works are evil!* can be earned by good works as well as evil; and therefore, as I have said, a prince is frequently forced to do evil, in order to maintain his position of power. For when that element of the population is corrupt— be it populace, soldiers or nobles—of which you deem that you have need in order to maintain yourself, you will have to follow their temper in order to satisfy it. In that case, then your good works will become your enemies.

But let us come now to the case of Alexander. He possessed a character so admirable that among other praises accorded him, it is noted that during the fourteen years he occupied the imperial throne, no one was ever put to death without due trial. Nevertheless, he was considered effeminate and a man who permitted himself to be governed by his mother. Thus he fell into disrepute, the army conspired against him, and he was murdered.

Turning, for the sake of contrast, to the characters of Commodus, Severus, and Antoninus Caracalla, these were all most cruel and rapacious men. In order to satisfy the soldiers, they became guilty of every injustice it was possible to inflict upon the people. And all of them, except Severus, came to a sad end. The latter possessed so much cunning and so many resources that managing at once to satisfy the soldiers and oppress the people, he enjoyed a happy reign. Those qualities of character caused a strange admiration in the people, leaving them stupified and incapable of reaction, while they delighted the soldiers who held him in great esteem. Considering the circumstance that he was a man new to the exercise of power, this man's achievements were very remarkable; so that I should like to point out briefly how well he knew how to play at once the fox and the lion, as I said above that a prince must [know]. When Severus learned of the ignominy of the Emperor, Julian, he persuaded his army, which was stationed in Slavonia, that it was his duty to go to Rome to avenge the death of Pertinax who had been put to death by the Praetorian Guards. Under this pretext and without revealing in any way his designs on the imperial power, he led his army toward Rome and he was already in Italy before his departure from Slavonia was suspected. On his arrival in Rome, the terrifed Senate elected him emperor and put Julian to death. After this beginning, two difficulties faced Severus: the first in Asia where Pescennius Niger, leader of the Asian armies had had himself proclaimed emperor; the second in the west, where Albinus, the commander there, also aspired to the imperial power. Severus realized that it was dangerous to show himself hostile to both these men at the same time, so he decided to attack Niger and deceive Albinus. To the latter he wrote that, as he had been elected emperor by the Senate, he wanted to share that dignity with him. He bestowed on him the title of Caesar and with the consent of the Senate associated Albinus with himself in the imperial power. Albinus accepted all these overtures at their face value. Once Severus had defeated Niger, however, and put him to death and had brought the eastern provinces under his own power, he returned to Rome and precipitated a quarrel with Albinus in the Senate. The ostensible reason was that Albinus, unmindful of the benefits he had received from Severus, had cunningly sought to kill him; it was necessary, he therefore argued, to proceed to punish that ingratitude.

Thereupon he set out to seek Albinus in France where he stripped him both of power and life. A detailed examination of the maneuvers of Severus shows him to have been at once a most ferocious lion and a most guileful fox. It will be noted that he was feared and held in awe by everyone, while maintaining the good will of the armies. Nor should it cause any wonder that he—a man new to power—should have been able to exercise so vast an authority, because his great reputation always protected him from the hatred which the people, by reason of his plunderings, might have conceived for him.

Antoninus, his son, was also in his own right a man of most excellent parts, a fact which made him an object of admiration to the people and most acceptable to the soldiers. He was a military man, able to sustain readily all the hardships attendant on that mode of life, one who despised delicate food and every other variety of luxury. These traits made him the idol of the armies. Nevertheless, his ferocity and his cruelty were so great and so beyond anything ever heard of that, after putting numerous individuals to death, he went on to cause a great part of the populace of Rome and the entire population of Alexandria to be executed. As a consequence, he became the most hated man in the world. He began to be feared even by his closest associates and ended by being murdered by a centurion, in the very presence of his troops. Here we should pause to note that princes cannot escape death at the hands of a fanatic; for anyone who has no fear of death himself can inflict it on another. Nevertheless, a prince ought not to be too much preoccupied with fear of such an event, for such assassinations are rare indeed. He should rather take care not to do grave injury to any of those who serve him or whom he has about him in the exercise of his power. Antoninus had done just that by putting to death in circumstances of disgrace the brother of that centurion and by insulting the latter with threats, while retaining him in his service. This kind of rash action must inevitably have caused him grief, as in the end it did.

Let us come now to Commodus. Retaining the imperial power should have been an easy thing for him, since he received it by hereditary right as the son of Marcus. All he had to do was to follow in his father's footsteps, and he would have satisfied the people and the soldiers alike. But he was of a cruel and bestial character; in order to satisfy his rapacity by plundering the people, he turned to indulging the soldiers, encouraging them in dissolute ways of life. In addition, he did not maintain his own dignity because he frequently descended into the theatres to do battle with the gladiators, and did other things as vile and as little worthy of the imperial majesty. This made him an object of contempt in the sight of his soldiers. Hated by one party and despised by the other, he soon became the object of a conspiracy and was murdered.

It remains for us to narrate the qualities of Maximus. He was a man of warlike temper and the armies, weary, as I noted above, of the effeminacies of Alexander, on the death of the latter elected him emperor. He did not enjoy that position very long, however, for two things combined to bring him into hatred and contempt: the one, his low origin, for he had once herded sheep in Thrace—a fact well known to everyone and a disgrace in the eyes of some; the other, the fact that, on his election, he put off going to Rome to be proclaimed emperor. Meanwhile he had earned a reputation for extreme cruelty, because of the actions carried out in his name by his prefects in

Rome and in other parts of the empire. Disdain for his low origins combined with hatred inspired by his cruelties, to fire rebellion first in Africa and then in the Senate and among the people of Rome. Finally all Italy rose up against him and his own army joined in the general revulsion, spurred by the aversion they had formed against him for his cruelties in the siege and sack of Aquileia. When they saw how many enemies he had, they lost their own fear of him and put him to death.

I do not wish to discuss Heliogabalus, Macrinus or Julian; all these men, having made themselves objects of contempt, were soon done away with. I would rather press on to the conclusion to be drawn from this discussion. The princes of our own day, I would submit, are less troubled by this necessity of satisfying the armed forces with extraordinary measures. They do indeed have to give these forces some consideration; but the problems they present are readily resolved, because princes today do not have standing armies which have become firmly entrenched in the government and administration of conquered territories like those of the Roman empire. If at that time it was necessary to satisfy the armies rather than the people, it was because the soldiers had more power than the people. Today, it is more necessary for all princes, except the Turk and the Sultan, to satisfy the people because the people have more power than the soldiers. I make exception of the Turk because he always has about him twelve thousand infantry and fifteen thousand cavalry upon which depend the security and strength of his reign. It is necessary for him, therefore, putting aside every other consideration, to maintain their friendship. In like manner the Sultan, since his administration is entirely in the hands of his soldiers, must, without regard to the people, maintain their obedience. It is also to be noted that the form of the Sultan's domain is different from that of all other principalities; it is somewhat like the Christian pontificate, which cannot be called either an hereditary or a new principality. The sons of the dead prince do not inherit his power; this passes to one elected by those who have the authority to do so. Since this institution is very old, it cannot be called a new principality because in it are to be found none of those difficulties which characterize new principalities. Though the prince is new, the institutions of that state are old and are prepared to receive him just as though he were an hereditary lord.

But let us return to our original subject. I submit that anyone who will review the discussion above will see that either hatred or disdain has been the cause of the downfall of the emperors mentioned above. He will also understand why it was that, a part of them proceeding in one fashion and the other part in another in each mode of procedure, one met a happy and another an unhappy end. It was useless for Pertinax and Alexander to want to imitate Marcus, because they were men new to power, while he held the imperial power by hereditary right. In like manner, it was a pernicious thing for Caracalla, Commodus and Maximinus to imitate Severus, because they did not have the innate capacity to follow in his footsteps. Therefore, a new prince in a new principality cannot imitate the actions of a Marcus, nor is it necessary for him to follow those of Severus. He ought to take from the model of Severus those aspects which are necessary for the establishment of his principality and from Marcus those which are necessary and conducive to the preservation of a state which, is already firmly established.

XX

*Whether the Construction of Fortresses and
Many Other Practices of Present-Day Princes
are Useful or Harmful*

Certain princes, in order to insure their position, have disarmed their subjects; others have fostered factions in the fortified towns which they have conquered. Others have purposely fostered animosities against themselves; still others have devoted themselves to winning over to themselves those who in the beginning of their reign were suspected of lack of attachment. Some have built fortresses; others have leveled and destroyed the same. And although it is impossible to give an uncontested opinion on all of these questions, unless one considers the particular conditions of each state in which one or another of these decisions was taken, still, I will discuss them in that inclusive manner which the material, taken in itself, invites.

It never has been the case, to be sure, that a new prince has disarmed his subjects; on the contrary, when he has found them unarmed, he has always armed them. The reason is clear. By arming your subjects you arm yourself. Those who have been under suspicion become loyal to you and those who were loyal before, now become from mere subjects, your partisans. Since all subjects cannot be armed, when those whom you arm are benefited thereby, you can deal with the rest with great firmness. When those whom you do arm recognize that you have dealt with them in a special manner, they will feel more obligated to you. And the remainder will excuse you, judging that it was necessary for you to act so, since the others had merited more through the graver dangers and responsibilities they had assumed. When, by contrast, you begin to disarm them, you begin to offend them, to show that you are diffident toward them, either because you are a coward or because you are suspicious. Whichever reason they assign will have the same effect: that of generating hatred toward you. Should this happen, since you cannot remain unarmed you will find yourself turning to mercenary troops, the quality of which has been described above. Mercenaries—no matter how expert they may be—will never prove so loyal that they will protect you from powerful enemies or suspicious subjects. Therefore, as I have said, a new prince in a new state has always organized military forces drawn from his subjects. The histories are full of examples of this. When, however, a prince acquires a new state which he adds to old possessions, he finds it necessary to disarm the new state—with the exception of those in it who have been your partisans. These, eventually, as time and occasion provide, must in their turn be rendered soft and effeminate. The situation must be such that all of the armed forces in your state are composed of your own soldiers, those who served under you in your older possessions.

Our ancestors and those who were thought to be experts in such matters, used to say that it was necessary to hold Pistoia by means of internal factions and Pisa by means of fortresses. For this reason they used to fan the differences among their subjects in the various fortified towns, in order in this way to maintain firmer control of them. In those days, when a certain balance of power existed in Italy it was possible to pursue such a policy with good results. I do not, however, believe that this can be taken as a precept today, because I do not believe that divisions thus fostered bring about satisfactory results. The opposite seems the case. When the enemy draws near, cities so divided will be lost immediately, because the weaker faction will always desert to external forces and the loyalty of the others cannot be retained.

The Venetians—moved, I believe, by the reasons mentioned above—fostered the Guelf and the Ghibelline factions in the cities subject to them. While they never permitted these rivalries to come to the point of bloodshed, they did foster them so that the citizens, occupied in these quarrels, could not unite against the Venetians. As we have seen, in the end this did not work out as they had planned; for when they were defeated at Vailà, one of those factions suddenly took fire and seized the entire state from the Venetians. Tactics such as these indicate weakness in a prince. Divisions such as these are never to be permitted in a strongly organized state; they are at best useful only in times of peace, for then they make it somewhat easier to control one's subjects. But when war comes the fallacy of such a policy is immediately made evident.

Without question, princes become great when they overcome the difficulties and oppositions which they encounter. Therefore when fortune has ordained the greatness of a new prince—for such have greater need than hereditary princes for acquiring a reputation—it raises up enemies against him, and encourages them to attack him, so that he may have the opportunity of overcoming them and, by the very ladder which they have provided, rise to a higher position. Many think that a sagacious prince ought—when opportunity offers—cunningly to encourage some enemy against himself, so that by crushing him, his own greatness may be enhanced.

Princes, and especially new princes, have discovered greater loyalty and greater utility in those men upon whom, at the beginning of their reign, they had looked with suspicion than in those who had seemed their trusted allies. Pandolfo Petrucci, Lord of Siena, used to administer his state more through those whom he had first held in suspicion than those on whom he had at first relied. Of this matter, it is not possible to speak securely in general terms, because it varies according to the temper of the subjects. I will limit myself to pointing out that a prince will never have any difficulty in winning over to himself those who at the beginning were hostile to him, when they are such as need someone to lean upon; they even become more efficient in his service when they realize that they have to cancel out that initial hostility by their present mode of conduct. In this way, the prince gets greater service from them, in the end, than from those who feel so secure in their position that they overlook his interests.

Since the matter demands it, I do not want to neglect reminding princes who have taken a new state through the favor of its inhabitants, to give careful consideration to the reasons which have moved those who favored them. If these have not been motives of natural affection toward himself, but rather of discontent toward the existing regime, he may find it most difficult to retain their allegiance because of the impossible demands they will make on him. Reviewing carefully the reasons for this, in the light of the examples which can be drawn from ancient and modern sources, he will conclude that it will be easier for him to gain to his side those who before were content with the existing state of affairs, and for this reason opposed him, than those who, because of their discontent, came forward as his friends and favored his occupation of the town.

It has been the custom of princes, in order to hold their states with greater security, to construct fortresses as a bridle and rein against those who might plan to rise against them, and as a safe refuge against sudden attack. I praise this tactic, because it has been employed since antiquity. Nevertheless, Niccolo Vitelli, in our own times, has destroyed the two fortresses in Città di Castello, in order to control that state better. Guido Ubaldo, Duke of Urbino, on returning to the domains from which he had been driven by Cesare Borgia, razed to their foundations all the fortresses of the province, thinking that without them it would prove more difficult to lose it again. The Bentivogli, on returning to Bologna, took similar steps. Fortresses may therefore be useful or otherwise, as the times vary. If they are beneficial to you under certain aspects, they may be harmful under others.

This question may be viewed in the following manner. The prince who has greater fear of his own people than of invaders ought to build fortresses; the one who has greater need to fear the invader ought not to do so. The Castle of Milan, built there by Francesco Sforza, has and will cause more trouble for the House of Sforza than any disorder in that state. The greatest of all fortresses remains the avoidance of the hatred of your people. Though you have many fortresses, while the people hate you the fortresses will not save you; for the people, once they have taken up arms, will never lack foreign supporters who will come to their aid. In our own day, it does not seem that fortresses have been of any use to any prince, with the possible exception of the Countess of Forlí.

On the death of her husband, Count Girolamo, she was able to withstand popular attack by retreating to the fortress, until aid from Milan could reach her and enable her to reestablish her power. Later on, however, her fortresses were of little help to her when Cesare Borgia assaulted the town; for the people within who were opposed to her immediately joined forces with the attacker.[35] Obviously, both at this time and on that earlier occasion it would have been more advantageous for her not to be hated by her people than to possess fortresses. All things considered, I praise those who construct fortresses and those who do not. But I blame any one who, trusting to his fortresses, thinks it a small matter that his people hate him.

XXI

How a Prince Ought to Govern to Gain Reputation

Nothing causes a prince to be esteemed so much as great undertakings and arresting exhibitions of his own abilities. We have in our own times, Ferdinand of Aragon, the present King of Spain. He can almost be considered a new prince; for he rose from the position of a weak king to become, for fame and glory, the first prince of Christendom. If you study his undertakings, you will find that they have all been on a very grand scale and some of them without parallel. At the opening of his reign, he attacked Granada. That campaign proved the foundation of his princely power.[36] He embarked on it without distraction and with no expectation of opposition. He employed it to engage the forces of the barons of Castile. So occupied, they were left little energy for innovations at home, and he thus gained dominion over them and esteem in their eyes, even while they were unaware that he was so employing them. He was able to use the monies of the Church and the taxes from his people to build up his army, and during that long war thus lay the foundations of that military force which was later to bring him so much honor. After this, in order to undertake still greater enterprises— always ostensibly in the name of religion—he assumed the pious but cruel task of expelling the Moors from his kingdom and despoiling them.[37] Never has there been seen a more pitiful nor more arresting enterprise. Under the same mantle of religion, he attacked Africa, undertook the Italian campaign, and finally turned his forces against France. Thus he was always engaged in the organization and execution of great undertakings which awakened astonishment and admiration in the souls of his subjects, and kept them in a constant state of expectation as to their outcome. Moreover, these undertakings followed so closely on the heels of each other that he has never allowed men, between one and the other [event], the necessary quiet to plot against him.

It also helps a prince very much to give similar striking examples of his capacity for internal government, as did Bernabò da Milano.[38] Thus whenever anyone does something out of the ordinary, whether for good or evil, he should be rewarded or punished in a manner which will cause a great deal of comment. Above all, a prince should seek every means to create in all his actions the image of himself as a great person of exceptional endowments.

A prince is also highly esteemed when he is a true friend or a true enemy; that is, when, without qualifications, he shows himself in favor of one party against another. Taking a stand is always better than being neutral. If two of your powerful neighbors come to blows, either they are such that, if one of them conquers, you will have reason to fear his victory, or they are not. In either of these cases it will be more useful for you to declare yourself and to wage wage war vigorously. If you do not declare yourself in the first case, you will always be the victim of the victor, to the pleasure and satisfaction of the loser; and you will have no justification for your action nor anyone to offer you refuge. The winner does not want dubious allies, who will not help him in difficulties. Nor will the loser receive you, for you did not offer, sword in hand, to share in his lot.

Antiochus had invaded Greece, invited there by the Aetolians, to drive out the Romans. He sent ambassadors to the members of the Achean league, who were friends of the Romans, counseling them to remain neutral. At the same time, the Romans were expending their efforts to persuade them to take up arms on their side. This matter came up for discussion before the council of the Achean league, where the ambassador of Antiochus presented his advice in favor of neutrality. The Roman legate replied, "The advice these men are giving you not to enter the contest, is most pernicious to your fortunes; if you do not intervene you will remain the prey of the victor, without dignity and without favor." [39]

It will always prove the case that the party which is unfriendly to you will seek your neutrality, while your friends will demand that you declare yourself by taking up arms. Princes who lack resolution, take the path of neutrality in order to avoid a present danger and for the most part find it the path to ruin. When, however, a prince declares himself boldly, in favor of one party or the other, his position possesses clear advantages. If the party with which he casts his lot wins—even though he is more powerful and you remain at his mercy—he is obligated to you and a friendship has been established. And men are never so without honor that, with such a display of ingratitude, they would then turn against you. Furthermore, victories are never such clear-cut things that the victor does not have to have some concern [and show] circumspection in his actions, especially in matters of justice. If, on the other hand, the one with whom you have allied yourself should lose, you will still be received by him. And to the degree that he can, he will help you and you will find yourselves linked in a fortune which may yet be retrieved. In the second case, when those who go to war with each other are such that you have nothing to fear in the outcome—however it may go—it is even greater prudence to declare your adherence clearly. For in this way, you contribute to the ruin of the one, with the aid of the other, who, were he really a wise man, would really be concerned to save the party he has destroyed. Your ally, if victorious, remains at your mercy. And it is impossible that, having your aid, he should not win.

Here it is to be noted that a prince ought never to throw in his lot with one more powerful than himself in an aggressive cause, unless sheer necessity compels him. In case of victory, he remains the prisoner of that stronger ally. And princes ought to avoid at all costs placing themselves at the mercy of others. The Venetians joined France against the Duke of Milan, though they were under no necessity of taking part in that campaign which was to prove their ruin. When it is not possible to avoid such a situation, as happened with the Florentines—when the pope and Spain sent their armies against Lombardy—the prince ought to declare himself, for the reasons mentioned. Nor should any state believe that it can enter into any such venture and alliance with complete assurances as to the outcome; rather, it ought always to consider carefully all the dubious possibilities. For this is the order of things. To avoid one danger without exposing oneself to another is impossible. Prudence consists rather in knowing how to weigh the various perils involved, and to choose the less harmful as the good.

A prince ought also to make it clear that he admires talent and is anxious to honor anyone for outstanding achievement. Further he ought to encourage his citizens and make it possible for them to exercise their skills, and to engage in trade and agriculture, and all the other professions which men cultivate. None of his subjects should be afraid to improve his possessions lest they be taken from him, nor be deterred by high taxes from engaging in some new venture in trade. On the contrary, he ought to provide rewards for those willing to undertake such things, and for everyone who in any way shows the desire to extend his city or increase his power. At suitable times of the year, he ought to provide entertainment for his people in the form of spectacles and festivities. Since every city is divided into various groups according to occupation or kinship, he ought to be aware of these groups and meet with them from time to time, giving them examples of his benevolence and munificence. At all times, and on all occasions, however, he should take care to maintain the dignity of his position which should never suffer diminution for any reason.

XXII

The Prince's Ministers

The election of his ministers is a matter of no little importance to a prince; for these will be good or bad according to the prudence he exercises in choosing them. The first criterion of the character of a prince is the kind of men he has about him. When they are loyal and capable, the prince may be judged wise; for he has known how to recognize their competence and their capacity for loyalty to himself. When they are of a lesser stamp, a negative opinion will be formed about him, too; for the basic error is his for having selected them.

Anyone acquainted with Antonio da Venafro, the minister of Pandolfo Petrucci, Lord of Siena, would immediately have recognized Petrucci as a most capable man because he had placed Antonio in that position. There are, it should be noted, three kinds of intelligence. The first understands matters directly by its own power, the second understands things when explained by another, and the third understands in neither the one way nor the other. The first is the most excellent, the second excellent indeed, the third entirely useless. One had necessarily to conclude of Pandolfo, that if he were not possessed of the first type, he certainly must have had the second. Any man who has the good judgment to recognize the good or evil in what another may say or do—though he himself lacks all power of invention—will be able to distinguish between the evil and the good actions of his ministers, and correct the first as he praises the second. The minister cannot hope to deceive such a man and consequently refrains from wrongdoing.

There is one way, however, by which a prince can come to understand and evaluate his ministers infallibly. When you see that a minister thinks more of himself than of you—that in all his activities he is pursuing some purpose of his own—you know that he cannot be a good minister of your affairs, and that you can never put your trust in him. The man who is entrusted with the administration of the state of another should never think of himself but of his prince, and should concern himself with nothing that does not pertain to the prince's interests. On the other hand, the prince, in order to remove his minister from temptation, ought to think about him—to honor him and make him rich—admit his obligations to him, and share with him both honors and responsibilities. In this way, the minister will recognize his dependence on and unity of interest with the prince; his abundant riches and numerous honors will prevent prevent his becoming greedy for more; and his many responsibilities will make him a natural enemy of change. When princes and their ministers enjoy mutual relations of this kind, they can confide completely in each other. When their relations are not of this kind, the end can only be disastrous for the one or the other.

XXIII

How Sycophants Must Be Shunned

I do not want to pass over unremarked a most important matter, an error against which princes can defend themselves only if they are exceedingly prudent and know how to choose their ministers very wisely. This is the matter of flatterers or sycophants, of which the courts of princes are full. Men take such satisfaction in their own affairs and so readily deceive themselves about them, that it is difficult for them to ward off these pests. Moreover, sometimes, in the process of defending yourself against them you may run the danger of incurring the contempt of some persons. The only way to protect yourself against the danger of adulations is to make men understand that they have nothing to fear from speaking the truth to you. On the other hand, when any one can speak his mind to you on any matter, he will tend to lose respect for you. A prudent prince will therefore pursue a third tactic. He will appoint only wise men to his government and allow only them free rein in speaking the truth to him; and then, moreover, only on those matters on which he chooses to consult them and on nothing else. On the other hand, he ought to subject them to careful questioning on all matters and to listen to their opinions carefully. After doing so, he ought to take counsel with himself and reach his own decisions. With his councils and with his ministers, his conduct should be such that they will understand that the more freely they speak, the more acceptable they will be to him. Except for these, he ought to listen to no one, try to penetrate beyond the matter being discussed, and remain firm in his own decisions. Anyone who acts otherwise, either acts precipitously under the influence of flatterers or is forever changing his mind with the changing appearances of things, both of which courses bring him to low esteem.

I would like in this connection to cite an example from our own times. Father Luca, emissary of Maximilian, the reigning Emperor, when speaking of his majesty, said that he never followed anyone's counsel and yet never did anything in the way that he himself wished. The reason was that he conducted himself in a manner quite the opposite of that which I have outlined above. The Emperor is a secretive man; wherefore he communicates his plans to no one and takes no advice concerning them. When he sets about putting them into effect, they become evident and known and are contradicted and opposed by those around him. This circumstance, as can readily be understood, diverts him from his purposes. As a result, what he does one day, he undoes the next. No one ever understands clearly what he plans or has in mind and no reliance can be placed on his decisions.

A prince should, obviously, always seek advice; but only when he wants it and not when others want to give it. Indeed, he should discourage anyone from offering him advice on any matter unless he shall have asked for it. For his own part, he should be a penetrating questioner and—concerning the questions he puts—a patient listener. When he realizes that some one, for one reason or another, is not telling him the truth, he should make his displeasure obvious. Many people have the impression that any prince who gives an appearance of wisdom, must do so because of the wise counsel he receives, and not because of his own endowment. In this they are doubtless mistaken. The general rule is this, and it never fails: a prince who is not himself a wise man, cannot be given good counsel—unless he has already by chance placed himself in the hands of some very prudent man who directs him in all matters. If such be the case, he may fare well, but the arrangement cannot endure for long; for that prudent director will in a short time take his power from him. When a prince, who is not himself a sagacious person, seeks counsel from more than one source, he will never receive concordant opinions nor will he himself know how to relate them. Of the men whom he consults, each will be thinking of his own interest, and the prince will not be able to counter this nor even perhaps recognize the fact. Matters cannot be otherwise. Men will always prove faithless to you unless they are made good by some necessity. Thus we must conclude that wise counsels, whatever their origin, must ultimately be born of the prudence of the prince, and not the prudence of the prince of good counsels.

XXIV

Why the Princes of Italy Have Lost Their States

The things which I have written above, prudently observed, make a new prince appear like one long established in power, make him immediately more secure and stable in his state than he would be had he ruled for a long time. A new prince is much more subject to scrutiny in all his actions than is an hereditary prince. And when those actions are recognized as manifesting great personal capacity, they are more powerfully attractive to men and engage their loyalty far more than does mere ancient lineage. For men are much more impressed by things of the immediate present than by events and claims of the past; and when they find present things good, they are content with them and do not look beyond. When satisfied with their present ruler, they will do all in their power to defend him, so long as he does not exhibit any deficiencies in himself. In this way he will acquire a double claim to glory: that of having founded a new principality and that of having adorned and strengthened it with good laws, a strong army, faithful allies and sound examples; just as one will have a double stigma of shame who, having been born a prince, has lost that state through lack of prudence.

If we now turn our attention to those Italian princes who in our own times have lost possession of their states, such as the King of Naples, the Duke of Milan[40] and others, they will be found to share a common weakness in military organization, judged according to the principles discussed above. Also, it will be found that some of them have alienated the people of their states, while others, though retaining the friendship of the people, did not know how to conciliate the interests of the nobles. This must be the case, for, except for these causes, states which have the capacity of placing an army in the field, are not lost. Philip of Macedon—not the father of Alexander but the man who defeated Titus Quintus—had little power in comparison with the Romans and the Greeks who attacked him. None the less, because he was a military man, he knew how to keep the people friendly to him and the nobles loyal, and was able to maintain hostilities for a number of years. Though in the end he lost control of certain cities, he did not lose his kingdom.

As a consequence, these princes of Italy, who had occupied their positions of power for many years, cannot accuse fortune of their subsequent loss; they must place the blame on their own lack of spirit. Never imagining in times of peace that things might change—a common failing this, in fair weather to take no account of an approaching storm—when evil times befell, they could think only of flight and not of how they might defend themselves. They nourished the hope that their peoples, growing weary of the insolence of the victors, might recall them. This policy is good when all else fails; but it was a grave mistake to have neglected all other means and placed all hope on this possibility. One does not fall, just in the hope that some one will help him to his feet again. It is possible that no one will; and if some one does, you will not find yourself secure, because your return was cowardly and not effected by yourself. Only those defenses are good, sure and dependable, which rest on yourself alone and your own resourcefulness.

XXV

How Far Fortune Prevails in Human Affairs and How She May Be Opposed

It is not unknown to me that many men have had and still entertain the view that the affairs of this world are so governed by fortune and by God that the prudence of men can have no effect upon them— indeed has no remedy against them. They convince themselves that there is no reason to worry much over events, but in all things it is better to permit oneself to be ruled by chance. This opinion has been the more readily acceptable in our own times because of the rapid changes in affairs which have been and are to be seen every day, frustrating all human conjecture. Indeed, in ruminating over these matters, I have sometimes found myself attracted to the same opinion. Nevertheless, I do not believe that our free will has been entirely extinguished. Therefore I am inclined to concede that fortune may well govern half of our actions, but that even fortune permits us to control, or at least influence, the other half. I compare fortune to one of those ruinous torrents, which, when they swell up, flood the plains, overturn trees and buildings, sweep earth from one place to deposite it in another. Everyone flees before them, everyone gives way to their onrush, powerless to oppose it in any way. Though men act in this way, still there is nothing else for them to do, when quiet returns, but to try to make some provision for the future, building barriers and dykes, so that when those waters rise again they may be directed into a canal or their onrush made less damaging and overwhelming. Thus it is with the movements of fortune, for fortune shows its power where there is no resourcefulness organized to resist it; it turns all its force against that point, where it knows that dykes and ramparts have not been erected to restrain it. If you consider Italy, which is the seat of all these changes and which has set them in motion, you will find her like an open countryside, without dykes and with no ramparts of any kind. Had she been protected by resourcefulness adequate to the need—as Germany, France and Spain have been—this inundation would not have worked such violent changes here, or perhaps would not have visited us at all. What I have said must suffice on the matter of opposing fortune in general.

Restricting my attention now to more particular conditions, I would note that we see a certain prince happy today, and tomorrow facing ruin without seeming to have changed in character or in any particular quality. I believe that this comes about, in the first place, through the causes which have been treated above at considerable length. The prince who places all his confidence in fortune will come to ruin when she fails him. I also believe that he is the fortunate prince who accommodates his tactics to the character of the times; and similarly, unfortunate is the one whose mode of procedure is out of step with them.

In the ends which they pursue, men proceed in different ways: one with circumspection, another impulsively; one with violence, another with artfulness and skill; one patiently, another impatiently. Still each of them, using different methods, can arrive at his goal. Again, of two men of circumspection, one achieves his purpose, the other does not. And likewise two are equally happy in the outcome, though pursuing different methods, the one circumspect, the other impetuous. All this results only from the quality of the times, to which their manner of proceeding conforms or fails to conform. This explains, as I have said, why two men acting in different ways can achieve the same goal, while of two men acting in the same way, one achieves his end and the other does not. This also explains why prosperity is subject to change. If one conducts himself with circumspection and patience—and these are what the times demand—he will be successful; however, if the needs of the times change, and he cannot alter his mode of conduct with them, he will be ruined. Nor is there to be found a man so prudent that he knows how to effect this accommodation; either because he cannot deviate from the direction in which his nature inclines him, or because, having heretofore always prospered while pursuing one method, he cannot persuade himself that he must now abandon it for another. Therefore the circumspect, when the time comes to act with force, does not know how to accommodate himself, and perishes. Had he known how to change his character with the times and the circumstances, his fortune would not have changed.

Pope Julius was impetuous in all his actions; but he found the times and course of events so in harmony with his mode of action that he nearly always realized happy results. Consider his first campaign against Bologna when Giovanni Bentivogli was still alive. The Venetians did not approve the undertaking, neither did the King of Spain; and at its outset Pope Julius was still disputing about it with France. Nevertheless, with his customary audacity and impulsiveness, he took personal command of the expedition.[41] That decision left Spain and the Venetians undecided and incapable of movement—the Venetians out of fear for the outcome, the King of Spain because of his ambition to regain the whole of the Kingdom of Naples. On the other hand, by it he forced the King of France to go along with him; for the King—seeing the Pope thus commit himself in the matter and desiring to retain his friendship in order eventually to humble the Venetians—felt that he could not deny him military support without doing him obvious injury. Julius, therefore, with his impetuous decision achieved what no other pontiff, exercising all possible human prudence, had been able to achieve. Had he delayed leaving Rome until all arrangements and negotiations had been concluded, as any other pontiff might have done, he never would have succeeded in this undertaking. The King of France would have offered a thousand excuses and the other parties involved would have aroused a thousand fears in him. I shall leave undiscussed his other enterprises, which were all marked with the same stamp and all succeeded just as well. The very brevity of his career in the pontificate, in fact, prevented him from ever knowing failure. But this can be said. Had the times ever demanded that he move with caution and circumspection, he would have met his ruin; for he never could have deviated from that mode of action to which his nature inclined him.

My conclusion is that, since fortune is fickle, while men persist in their modes of conduct, the event is happy when these happen to be in agreement, unhappy when they are at odds with each other. My own studied judgment is this: that it is better to be impetuous than circumspect; for fortune is a woman, and one must beat her and coerce her to keep her submissive. It is obvious that she permits herself to be conquered more readily by those who act in this way than by those who try to circumvent her by cold calculation. And since she is a woman, she always favors the young, for they are less circumspect and more ferocious, commanding her with greater boldness.

XXVI

An Exhortation to Liberate Italy from the Barbarians

Reflecting upon all the matters discussed above, there arose to my mind the question whether in present day Italy the times might not be right for the emergence of a new prince; and whether the situation might not be such as to offer a prudent and resourceful man the opportunity of introducing here a new political dispensation, which might at once do honor to him and bring great benefit to its entire population. My conclusion has been that so many circumstances now tend to favor a new prince, that I am unable to say when the times were ever more propitious. If, as I have suggested above,[42] it was necessary, in order that the powers of Moses might be revealed, that the people of Israel should undergo slavery in Egypt; that the Persians should be oppressed by the Medes, so that the greatness and courage of Cyrus might be made known; that the Athenians be dispersed, so that the excelling power of Theseus might be brought to light; then it was surely necessary that Italy should be reduced to the extremes in which she now finds herself—more enslaved than the Egyptians, more oppressed than the Persians, her unity more shattered than that of the Athenians; without leaders, without law, crushed, despoiled, lacerated, overrun; made to bear every sort of desolation. And although a man has already appeared in whom there was such a spark that one could rightly believe that he had been ordained by God for her redemption, it has also been seen how later, in the full tide of his most important conquests, he was rejected by fortune.[43] So now Italy remains lifeless, expectant of the coming of him who might heal her wounds; who might put an end to the dissection and plundering of Lombardy, to the exploitation and the extortion of the realm and of Tuscany, and might cure her of those wounds which so long have been festering. It may be seen how she prays God that he might send her someone who might redeem her from these barbarous outrages and cruelties. It can also be seen that she is entirely ready and disposed to follow some banner, if only one would be raised aloft. Nor is it possible to see in whom, in her present circumstances, she might place her hope more than in your illustrious House,[44] which by right of its fortune and its prowess, the favor shown it by God and the Church, whose present head comes from its members, might take in hand this work of renewal. This would not seem a very difficult undertaking, if you recall the lives and the achievements of the men we have spoken of in the course of our discussion. Although those men were rare and a cause of wonder, still they were men; and none of them was presented with an opportunity greater than that which exists today. Their undertakings were neither easier nor more just than this, nor did God favor them more than He favors you. In this cause is the greatest justice, "for war is just when it is necessary, and the arms in which resides a final hope are holy arms." *Justum enim est bellum quibus necessarium et pia arma ubi nulla nisi in armis spes est.*[45] Here is the greatest readiness of spirit, and when the spirit is ready, there can be no great obstacle—if only your House takes as its models those whom I have held up for your admiration. Here, moreover, are to be seen wonders greater than any worked by God before. The sea is opened; a cloud has shown the way; the stone has gushed forth water and manna rained down. Everything has conspired to your greatness. The rest remains for you to do. God does not want to effect it all, so as not to deny us our freedom of will and that part of the glory which belongs to us.

Nor is it a matter of wonder that none of the Italians whom I have mentioned [46] has been able to achieve what may be hoped for from your House. If in the midst of so many revolutions and the great movement of so many military enterprises, our military prowess has seemed to be extinguished, the reason is that the ancient methods were ineffective and no one has appeared with the genius to devise new ones. Nothing does more honor to the man newly risen to power, than the new laws and institutions which he introduces. When these are well founded and when they have the mark of greatness on them, they make him an object of reverence and admiration. And Italy offers both matter and occasion for the renewal of all institutions. Great are the reserves of strength in the members when the leaders are not lacking. Notice how, in duels and in combats engaging limited numbers, the Italians exhibit superiority in force, dexterity, ingenuity. When it comes to the combat of armies, however, they do not bear up under comparison. This results from the weakness of their leaders. Men without competence are obeyed and every one pretends to a knowledge he does not possess. Up to this time no one has appeared among us with so clear a superiority and a gift for leadership that the others will make way for him. Consequently for a long time and in the many wars waged over the last twenty years, every army composed entirely of Italians has given a poor account of itself. For evidence one need but cite Taro, and later, Alexandria, Capua, Genoa, Vailà, Bologna and Mestri.[47]

If your illustrious House wishes therefore to follow those excellent men who wrought the redemption of their countries, it is necessary before all else—and as the true foundation of every future campaign—to organize armies of native forces. For it is impossible to find more loyal, truer or more competent soldiers. Individually excellent, together they will become even better when they see at their head their own prince, and when in turn they are honored and esteemed by him. It is also necessary to prepare these armies in order, by our own Italian initiative, to defend ourselves from external enemies. Though the Swiss and Spanish infantries are both accounted terrifying, nevertheless, both suffer from a common deficiency, by the exploitation of which a third force might not only oppose, but even overcome them. The Spanish cannot withstand cavalry, while the Swiss retreat before infantry forces which are as obstinate in combat as themselves. Thus it has been proved—and it will be proved again, if tried—that the Spaniards cannot withstand French cavalry while the Swiss are shattered by Spanish infantry. Although there has been no really compelling evidence of this latter, there was afforded a glimpse of it in the battle of Ravenna, when the Spanish infantry confronted the German infantry which employs the same formations as the Swiss. The Spaniards, with great bodily agility and under the protection of their bucklers, penetrated the array of German pikes, between and beneath, inflicting damage against which the Germans were helpless. If the cavalry had not intervened, the Spaniards would have slain them all. By correcting the defects observed in these two infantry forces, it would be possible to organize on new principles, one which would be able to resist cavalry and have no fear of other infantry formations. This could be effected through improved quality of arms and alterations of the formations. It is innovations of this kind which win a new prince reputation and stature.

This great opportunity ought not, therefore, to be permitted to escape. Italy, after so long a period of desolation, should at last see her redeemer. Nor can I express the affection with which he would be received in all those provinces which have suffered those foreign inundations, with what thirst for revenge, with what loyalty and resolution, with what devotion and tears! What doors would be closed to him? Who would refuse him obedience? What jealousy would dare oppose him? What Italian deny him recognition? This foreign domination is a stench in the nostrils of all. Let your illustrious House therefore put its hand to this undertaking with the spirit and the hope with which just causes may always rightly be undertaken, so that, beneath your standard, our country may be restored to its noble position and under your auspices the utterance of Petrarch may be realized:

> Virtù contra furore
> Prenderà l'arme e sia 'l combatter corto.
> Che l'antico valore
> Nell' Italici cor non é ancor morto.[48]

> Virtue will take up arms against the fury
> And the battle will be brief
> For the ancient valor
> Is not yet dead in Italian hearts.

1-7-64

NOTES

1. Probably in *Discorsi,* I.
2. Treaty of Bagnolo in 1482; he seized Ferrara in 1510 with French help.
3. "Toothing-stone" (Italian "addentellato")—an irregularity in a wall which enables a continuation of it to be constructed. The figure is probably unique with Machiavelli although the historian Varchi Istorie, II, uses a somewhat similar one.
4. In October of 1511, on the initiative of Julius II, the Holy League between Spain, Venice and the Papacy was formed with the purpose of driving the French out of Italy. The decisive engagement of the war was the battle of Ravenna (April 11, 1512); although victorious, the French were forced to withdraw because of the loss of their leader, Gaston de Foix.
5. Greece, i.e., the whole of the Balkan peninsula, was conquered by the successive incursions of Murad II, Mohamet II, Bajazet and Selim, culminating in the capture of Constantinople with which the establishment of the Turkish power in Europe became an accomplished fact in 1453.
6. Machiavelli is not wholly in accordance with historical records in this assertion.
7. The events to which Machiavelli refers in this passage occured between 200 and 189 B.C.
8. Pope Alexander VI of the House of Borgia had newly reaffirmed the temporal power of the Church and had set on foot, through the instrumentality of his son, Cesare Borgia, a policy of penetration and domination in central Italy (cf. infra Chapter XI). The Venetians were feared by all the other Italians on account of their tireless efforts to extend their power on the mainland of Italy, in the direction of Lombardy and the Romagna and even into southern Italy through Brindisi and other ports. For this the chief authority is the historian, Guicciardini, *History of Italy,* I,1.
9. Louis XII of France obtained from Pope Alexander VI the dissolution of his marriage with Jeanne, daughter of Louis XI and sister of Charles VIII; his purpose was to clear the way for his marriage with the widow of Charles VIII, Anne of Brittany, to secure dominion of that dukedom. The Pope further

favored the king by granting the rank of cardinal to Georges d'Amboise, the king's counselor. Cesare Borgia had shed the cardinal's robes and had obtained the titles of Count of Valence and Duke of Valentinois, whence he was popularly called "Il Valentino."

10. The Empire, which was to have been governed after the death of Alexander by seven Greek generals, was immediately shaken by the contests which arose among them; his vast conquests were then dismembered into eleven kingdoms among which the most important were Egypt, Syria, and Macedonia.

11. That is, forcing them to take refuge in fortified positions and to abandon the open countryside.

12. In the civil wars which shook the last century of republican Rome, the provinces frequently took sides with one or another of the contending powers; thus Spain, Greece and the East were for Pompey and against Caesar.

13. The choice of representative figures has led many to point out that Machiavelli is quite indifferent to the real historical value of his examples and considers chiefly the use to which he puts them; thus Manzoni, the novelist and critic, in his famous essay, *On the Historical Romance,* writes: "Machiavelli so vigilant and profound an observer, among so many various observations, makes none which is truly historically critical. . . . It is this indifference for the positive reality of historical facts, this immediate seizure by the mind of those things which may have value merely because of verisimiltude . . . which may be noted in a man of his great capacity. . . ."

14. The quotation is from the *History* of Justin which was an important source for Machiavelli. The precise words are: "ut nihil ei regium deesse praeter regnum videretur," Justin, *History,* XXIII,4.

15. At Magione, a village near Perugia, a league against Cesare Borgia was formed October 9, 1502 by the Orsini, the Bentivoglio and others who stood in danger from his ambitions.

16. The authority for this account is Guicciardini, *History of Italy,* VI,4.

17. Agathocles, tyrant of Syracuse, Sicily (316-389 B.C.), and from 304 B.C., king of Greek Sicily, and not, as Machiavelli implies, of the entire island. Singlehanded, he threatened the power of Carthage in Africa.

18. Machiavelli traveled through Switzerland and spent some time in the Tyrol, between January and June of 1508, as legate from the Republic of Florence to

Emperor Maximilian. He never visited Germany proper, though he often speaks of it with admiration, and with admirable clarity of judgment.

19. The allusion is to the League of Cambrai of 1508 in which Pope Julius II, the Emperor Maximilian and Ferdinand the Catholic participated.

20. "Consider how many wars there have been in Italy since the death of King Charles to the present; wars habitually make men belligerent and win them reputations; but these, because they were greater and fiercer, brought loss of reputation to their participants and to their captains. This convinces one that the habitual ways of conducting warfare were not enough. . . ." Machiavelli, *The Art of War,* VII.

21. Machiavelli enlarges upon the failings of Italian princes which weakened them for war in *The Art of War,* VII.

22. After occupying Bologna, Julius II had in mind also to seize Ferrara; but he was turned back by Alfonso d'Este and the French forces. Even more, he was forced to give up Bologna as well. His fortunes improved only when he formed the "Holy League" with Ferdinand the Catholic in 1511.

23. John Cantacuzene, in his dynastic struggle with the Paleologi, in 1346 formed an alliance with the Sultan of Turkey who sent forces to the support of the emperor; this provided the Turks with their first foothold in Europe, which served as the basis for further penetration and expansion.

24. The first time under the Emperor Valensein in 376 A.D.; later and in greater numbers under Theodosius in 382 A.D.

25. The quotation is from the Roman historian Tacitus, *Annals,* XIII,13. The exact phrasing is "Nihil rerum mortalium tam instabile ac fluxum est quam fama potentiae non sua vi nixae."

26. Among others, Plato in the *Republic;* Machiavelli is here thinking perhaps of the many adulatory compositions of contemprorary humanists in praise of particular rulers and constitutions to which they ascribed model status.

27. This view is echoed by Guicciardini in his treatment of Pope Julius. Cf. his *History of Italy,* VI,v.

28. Louis XII of France.

29. Ferdinand the Catholic.

30. Virgil, *Aeneid* I, 563-564.

31. Locri Epizyphiria, a city in Sicily, was sacked and put to flames by Q. Pleminius, the propraetor whom Scipio had left in Sicily; Scipio did not chastise him

but contented himself with disciplining certain military tribunes.

32. The allusion is perhaps to Dante, *Inferno,* XXVII, 72-75, where Guido da Montefeltro says to Dante:

Mentre ch'io forma fui d'ossa e di polpe
che la mia madre mi diè, l'opere mie
non furon leonine, ma di volpe.

While I still bore the form of bone and flesh
My mother gave me, my works
Were not like those of the lion, but of the wolf.

33. This body began to function with the name of "Parliament of France" or "Parliament of Paris" under Louis IX about 1254; it was more firmly established and given a fixed seat in Paris by Philip in 1302; the latter also added to it the "third estate" thus modifying its original feudal constitution.

34. From Marcus Aurelius to Maximinius, that is, from 161-238 A.D.

35. The population of Forlí rebelled on December 15, 1499; the countess took refuge in the castle which was assailed by Valentino (Borgia) who arrived there on the 19th. On January 12, 1500, the fortress fell and the woman whom the historian Guicciardini calls "great-spirited and of manlike courage" lost her throne, *History of Florence,* XXI.

36. After ten years of continuous seige and assault, Granada fell to Ferdinand January 12, 1492, thus completing the unification of Spain.

37. That is, the Moors and the Jews who were ostensibly converted to Catholicism, but remained secretly faithful to their old religions.

38. Barnabò Visconti, shared the lordship of Milan with his relatives Matteo and Galeazzo from 1354; after the death of the latter he ruled alone in 1378. He was deposed in 1385 by his nephew Gian Galeazzo, who, though a man of extreme cruelty, was a capable politician and administrator and strengthened the position of the Visconti in Milan.

39. The quotation is from Titus Livius, XXXV,48. The exact words are: "Nam, quod optimum esse dicant, non interponi vos bello, nihil tam vanum, immo tam alienum rebus vestris est; quippe sine gratia, sine dignitate, praemium victoris eritis."

40. The King of Naples; that is, Ferdinand of Aragon (cf. Chapter I). The Duke of Milan, that is, Ludovico Moro (cf. Chapter III).

41. Cf. the account in Chapter XI.

42. Cf. the account in Chapter VI.

43. Cesare Borgia, Duke of Valentinois.
44. The House of Medici, which then ruled in Florence
    in the person of Lorenzo, to whom the work is dedi-
    cated; and the Papacy in the reign and person of
    Leo X.
45. Titus Livius, IX,1: "Justum est bellum quibus neces-
    sarium et pia arma quibus nulla nisi in armis relin-
    quitur spes."
46. Cesare Borgia and Francesco Sforza.
47. The battles referred to are: Fornovo al Taro, 1495;
    Alexandria, beseiged by the French, 1499; Capua,
    which fell to the French in 1501; Genoa which fell
    to Louis XII in the spring of 1507; Bologna, aban-
    doned by the papal legate and taken by the French in
    1511; Mestri, the Spanish against the Venetians,
    1513; for Vailà cf. Chapter III above.
48. These lines close Strophe VI of the "Canzone"
    ("Italia mia, benchè il parlar sia indarno") of the
    poet Petrarch, often mentioned by Machiavelli.

GLOSSARY OF NAMES

(Only those names important in Machiavelli's text or used as examples are noted.)

ACUTO, GIOVANNI, Italian form of the name of the Englishman, John Hawkwood, who became after 1360 a leader of mercenary troops in Italy.

AGATHOCLES, Became ruler of Syracuse in 317 B.C. Machiavelli's account of him would seem to have been taken from the Roman historian, Justin.

ALEXANDER, THE GREAT, 356-323 B.C., king of Macedonia.

ALEXANDER, M. Aurelius Alexander Severus, Roman Emperor (222-235 A.D.).

ALEXANDER VI, Pope (1492-1503); before his election to the papacy Cardinal Rodrigo Borgia.

ANTIOCHUS, THE GREAT, King of Syria (223-187 B.C.).

ASCANIO, Cardinal Ascanio Sforza.

BAGLIONI, Name of a ruling family of Perugia in the 15th century.

BENTIVOGLIO, Name of a ruling family in Bologna.

———, Annibale, murdered in 1455.

———, Giovanni, 1438-1508.

BERGAMO, BARTOLOMMEO DA, Named Colleone, mercenary in service of Venice after 1424; died 1475.

BORGIA, CESARE, 1476-1507, Duke of Valentino; son of Rodrigo Borgia and Vanozza Catanei; Renaissance "empire builder" under the aegis of his father who reigned as Pope Alexander VI.

BRACCIO, Name of a family of mercenary leaders, the most noted of whom was Andrea, 1368-1424, called da Montone.

CANNESCHI, Name of a noble family of Bologna.

CARACALLA, M. Aurelius Antoninus, Roman Emperor (211-217 A.D.).

CHARLES VII, 1403-61, King of France.

CHARLES VIII, 1470-1498, King of France.

COLONNA, Name of a ruling family of mediaeval and

Renaissance Rome; the chief figure mentioned by Machiavelli, Cardinal Antonio, died in 1508.

EPAMINONDAS, Fourth century B.C. Theban general and stateman.

FABIUS MAXIMUS, Roman consul and dictator, died 203 B.C.

FERDINAND OF ARAGON, 1452-1516, King of Aragon and of Castile, the latter through his marriage with Isabella of Castile; effected final eviction of the Moors through the conquest of Granada. In Italy, he secured dominion of the entire southern portion of the peninsula and of Sicily.

FERRARA, Duke of, Ercole d'Este; ruled Ferrara (1471-1505).

FILIPPO, Duke, Filippo Visconti, Duke of Milan (1412-1447); last of his line; united his house with that of Sforza through the marriage of his daughter Bianca Maria to Francesco Sforza.

FORLÌ, Caterina Sforza 1463-1509, Countess of; retained power in Forlì after the assassination of her husband, Girolamo Riario, count of Forlì, in 1488 until the capture of the town by Cesare Borgia in 1500.

GUIDOBALDO, 1472-1508, Duke of Urbino; last duke of the Montefeltro line. Fled Urbino in 1502 before Cesare Borgia; returned when Cesare's mercenary troops rebelled. The *Book of the Courtier* of Baldessare Castiglione was written under his patronage and depicted life at his court.

HAMILCAR, Barca, commander of the Catharginian forces in Sicily during the First Punic War (264-241 B.C.).

HANNIBAL, 247-183 B.C., son of Hamilcar; commander of the Carthaginian forces after 221 B.C. Invaded Italy by way of the Alps in the Second Punic War, but failed to take Rome.

HIERO, of Syracuse, Hiero II; elected ruler of that city in 270 B.C. upon the defeat of the Mamertines. Allied himself first with the Carthaginians but later with Rome.

JOANNA (GIOVANNA) II, Queen of Naples (1414-1435), lost that kingdom to the forces of Ferdinand of Aragon.

JULIAN, M. Didius, created emperor by the Praetorian guard on the death of Pertinax in 193 A.D.

JULIUS II, Pope (1503-1513); Giuliano della Rovere, Cardinal of San Pietro ad Vincula before his ascent of the papal throne. Laid the foundations for the present Basilica of St. Peter.

LEO X, Pope (1513-1521); Cardinal Giovanni dei Medici, son of Lorenzo the Magnificent.

LOUIS XI, King of France (1461-1483); greatly extended the territory of the French crown.

LOUIS XII, King of France (1498-1515); son of Charles of Orléans; conducted military operations in Italy with the object of subjecting that peninsula, but did not succeed in this project.

LUDOVICO, 1476-1500, Duke of Milan called il Moro; lost the dukedom to Louis XII in 1499; but recovered it in 1500, only to be defeated by a fresh French army; died under French imprisonment.

MACRINUS, M. Opilius, Roman emperor (217-218 A.D.); defeated by the supporters of Heliogabalus and Salin.

MANTUA, Francesco Gonzaga, Marquis of, commander of Italian forces at battle of Fornovo in 1495; renowned *condottiere*.

MARCUS AURELIUS (M. Aurelius Antoninus), Roman emperor (161-180 A.D.); called the philosopher for his loftly expression of Stoic ideals in the *Meditations*.

MAXIMILIAN, 1459-1519, of Hapsburg; elected Holy Roman emperor in 1486 but was never crowned; in 1508 assumed title of emperor-elect with consent of Julius II. Devoted his efforts to strengthening Hapsburg influence and power.

MAXIMINUS, C. Julius Verus, Roman emperor (235-238 A.D.); slain by his own troops.

OLIVEROTTO, of Fermo, family name, Euffreducci; the events which Machiavelli discusses took place in 1501. He was killed by Cesare Borgia at Sinigaglia in 1502.

ORCO, Ramirro de, Ramior de Lorqua; lieutenant of Cesare Borgia; appointed governor of Romagna in 1501 by him; killed 1502.

ORSINI, Family of the; rose to influence in Rome in the

13th century; leaders of mercenary soldiers, in which capacity they were engaged by Cesare Borgia.

————, Paulo, leader of the Orsini faction, until he was killed by Cesare Borgia at Sinigaglia in 1502.

PERTINAX, P. Helvius, Roman emperor for a few months in 193 A.D.; killed by mutinous troops.

PETRARCA, Francesco, 1304-1374, one of the greatest of Italian poets; the lines with which Machiavelli closes the Prince are from his Canzone XVI: "Italia mia. . . ."

PETRUCCI, Pandolfo, become ruler of Siena in 1502.

PHILOPOEMEN, general of the Achaean league, elected to that post in 208 B.C.

PITIGLIANO, Niccolò Orsini, Count of, 1442-1510; mercenary leader, commanded for the Venetians at the disastrous battle of Vailá.

ROUEN, Georges d'Amboise, 1460-1510, archbishop of Rouen; Cardinal in 1498.

SAN GIORGIO, Raffaello Riario of Savona, Cardinal with the title of San Giorgio.

SAVONAROLA, Girolamo, 1452-1498, Dominican friar, prior of San Marco convent in Florence. After 1491, by his prophetic and denunciatory preaching, he secured a large political following. After the expulsion of the Medici his influence reached its zenith during the years 1494-97. He was the prime shaper of the republican constitution of 1494. However, he incurred the hostility of Pope Alexander VI and after 1498 his influence quickly waned. In that year he was imprisoned, tortured and executed.

SCIPIO, P. Cornelius, 234-183 B.C., called Africanus; Roman commander who achieved victory over Hannibal in Spain. Subject of the famous "Dream of Scipio" in the De Re Publica of Cicero.

SEVERUS, L. Septimus, Roman emperor (193-211 A.D.)

SFORZA, Cardinal Ascanio, brother of Ludovico Moro; captured by the French in 1500.

————, Muzio, Attendolo, 1369-1424, founder of the fortunes of that house; a condottiere by profession; killed in the service of Queen Joanna (Giovanna) of Naples.

————, Francesco, 1401-1466, son of Muzio (see above); like his father, a *condottiere;* he entered the service of Filippo Visconti, Duke of Milan, and married his daughter, Bianca Maria. On the death of Visconti, he seized the duchy for himself.

SIXTUS V, Pope (1417-1484), Francesco della Rovere; uncle of Giuliano della Rovere who ruled as Julius II.

VITELLI, The, a family of *condottieri.*

————, Niccolo, Ruler of Città di Castello; died in 1486.

————, Paolo, a mercenary in the service of Florence against Pisa.

————, Vitellozzo, killed by Cesare Borgia at Sinigaglia in 1502.

SUGGESTED READINGS

BOOKS

Butterfield, Herbert. *The Statecraft of Machiavelli*. London, 1955.

Chabod, Federico. *Machiavelli and the Renaissance*. London, 1958.

Gilbert, A. H. *Machiavelli's Prince and Its Forerunners*. Durham, 1938.

Ritter, Gerhard. *The Corrupting Influence of Power*. London, 1952.

Strauss, Leo. *Thoughts on Machiavelli*. Glencoe, 1958.

Whitfield, J. H. *Machiavelli*. Oxford, 1957.

ESSAYS

Burd, Lawrence. "The Renaissance Prince," *Machiavelli*. Heath, 1960.

Burnham, James. "The Science of Power," *The Machiavellians*. New York, 1943.

Butterfield, Herbert. "Machiavelli's Historical Method and Statecraft," *Machiavelli*. Heath, 1960.

Chabod, Federico. "The Synthesis and Condemnation of Italian History," *Machiavelli*. Heath, 1960.

Croce, Benedetto. "The Autonomy and Necessity of Politics," *Machiavelli*. Heath, 1960.

Gilbert, Felix. "The Nationalism of Machiavelli," *Machiavelli*. Heath, 1960.

Laski, Harold J. "Machiavelli and the Present Time," *Dangers of Obedience and Other Essays*. New York, 1938.

Meinecke, Friedrich. "Raison d'Etat in Machiavelli," *Machiavelli*. Heath, 1960.

Praz, Mario. "Machiavelli and the Elizabethans," *The Flaming Heart*. London, 1958.

ARTICLES

Arciniegas, G. "Savonarola, Machiavelli and Guido Antonio Vespucci," *Political Science Quarterly*, LXIX (1954), 184-201.

Burns, E. M. "The Liberalism of Machiavell," *The Antioch Review,* VIII (1948), 121-130.

Gilbert, Felix. "The Humanist Concept of the Prince and *The Prince* of Machiavelli," *Journal of Modern History,* XI (1939), 449-483.

————. "On Machiavelli's Idea of 'Virtu'," *Renaissance News,* IV (1952), 53-55.

Gilbert, Gilbert. "Political Thought of Renaissance and Reformation," *Huntington Library Quarterly,* IV (1941), 443-468.

Hexter, J. H., " 'Il Principe' and 'Lo Stato'," *Studies in the Renaissance,* IV (1957), 113-138.

Senemo, Renzo. "A Falsification by Machiavelli," *Renaissance News,* XII (1959), 159-167.

Strauss, Leo. "Machiavelli's Intention: The Prince," *American Political Science Review,* LI (1957), 13-40.

Voegelin, Eric. "Machiavelli's Prince: Background and Formation," *Review of Politics,* XIII (1951), 142-168.

Whitfield, J. H. "The Politics of Machiavelli," *Modern Language Review,* L (1955), 433-443.

————. "Machiavelli's Use of 'Ordini'," *Italian Studies,* X (1955), 236-244.

7. Strong despot is needed to found
   the state, and to reform it
   when it is corrupted
   a. His power will "wither away" into
      legal self govt.
Nobility are opposed to both to ruller & to
   middle class ∴ must be extirpated
   a. Strong hatred for mercenary soldiers
above all, nat'l patriotism overrides every
   other duty
   a. more emotional than rational

J. Herman Randall, Jr. *The Career of Philosophy*
New York: Columbia, 1962

"There is irony in machiavelli's
anticlericalism and anti-Christian polem
For he is really agreeing with the
augustinian theory of government as
necessary after the Fall because of
the corruption of man's nature: only
civil authority can keep original
sin in check." p 135

B
M 25 M

___

M's political philosophy:

1. Human nature essentially egostic & selfish
2. Security possible only thru strong gov't & law
   (cf. Hobbes)
3. conflict is normal: in a healthy society interests
   are held in equilibrium
4. Everything depends on the lawgiver & the way his
   laws mold nat'l character
   a. only law holds selfish men together
5. Ruler is outside morality as its sou—
   a. Emphasis on will of God in Scotist &
      ochamise theol. has been naturalized into
      the will of the prince
6. But not political absolutism — and advocate
   for free self-governing people. (Greek)